Landscapes of
PORTUGAL
(ALGARVE)

a countryside guide

Brian and Eileen Anderson

SUNFLOWER
BOOKS

*Dedicated to Barry and Doreen Boothman,
in recognition of their steadfast support*

First published 1991 by
Sunflower Books
12 Kendrick Mews
London SW7 3HG, UK

ISBN 0-948513-80-2

Important note to the reader _____

We have tried to ensure that the descriptions and maps in this book are
error-free at press date. The book will be updated, where necessary,
whenever future printings permit. It will be very helpful for us to receive
your comments (sent in care of the publishers, please) for the updating of
future printings. We also rely on those who use this book — especially
walkers — to take along a good supply of common sense when they
explore. Conditions change fairly rapidly in Algarve, and *storm damage
or bulldozing may make a route unsafe at any time.* If the route is not as
we outline it here, and your way ahead is not secure, return to the point of
departure. *Never attempt to complete a tour or walk under hazardous
conditions!* Please read carefully the notes on pages 47 to 55, as well as
the introductory comments at the beginning of each tour and walk
(regarding road conditions, equipment, grade, distances and time, etc.).
Explore *safely*, while at the same time respecting the beauty of the
countryside.

Photographs by the authors
Maps adapted by John Theasby and Pat Underwood, with permission of
the Instituto Geográfico e Cadastral, Lisbon
Drawings by Frances Winder
Printed and bound in the UK by KPC Group, Ashford, Kent

E/AJ

Contents

4   Landscapes of Portugal (Algarve)

Tiled fountain at Fonte Grande, Alte

 Preface

Legend tells of how a Moorish king married a Scandinavian beauty and brought her to Algarve. She loved to watch the sun's rays seeking out and painting the hilltops in hues of evening gold. But when the summer season faded through autumn into winter, she became deeply unhappy and pined longingly for the snows of her native land. Worried at the unhappy state of his beloved, the king arranged for thousands and thousands of almond trees to be planted throughout the region. Even now, in January and February, the land is dusted with a covering of almond blossom in delicate shades of pink and white lying like a soft fall of snow, filling the hollows and outlining the hillsides.

Below the 'snow' lies a carpet of burnished gold, as the Bermuda buttercups burst into bloom to announce the arrival of spring. Oranges fill the trees; iris, bluebells, and even the insect-mimicking wild orchids follow in abundance. 'Is this the same Algarve', you may ask, 'as the Algarve of high-rise hotels, fine beaches and a coastline so famous that there is no need to look further?' Such is the beauty of the coastline, that few visitors look for more — but we did. We found a countryside full of interest and beauty, quietly awaiting discovery. From flowers and fountains, hilltops and history, to windmills and watermills, we can set your feet wandering to find them all. There are car tours, too, to get you out and about, searching out little-known points of interest — like the huge rose compass (*rosa dos ventos*) on the barren promontory of Sagres, where Prince Henry the Navigator founded his school of navigation, or the Moorish castle and old Roman bridge at Paderne.

But don't think for one moment that we have turned our backs on and ignored the beautiful and rugged western coastline. Wherever it is still unspoilt and free from development, we have incorporated it into a walk. Some of the finest and most picturesque coastline in Algarve is yours to share only with others who are happy to tread the coastal paths. There are quieter bays, too, where you can take a break from walking, for a relaxing dip in the sea and perhaps a refreshing glass of well-chilled *vinho verde* before stepping out to complete the walk.

5

Some days are made for relaxing, so why not try a country picnic? We have included a variety of picnic suggestions, many involving only a short walk. Some are set in country villages — like the one at Alte, which gives you a chance to explore an old settlement and enjoy a short stroll by the riverside, before settling down to your picnic lunch. Or perhaps you feel ready for the hustle and bustle of a country market. Here you can feel the excitement of the locals, share the life, the colour, the customs and culture for a few short hours before it all fades to empty stalls.

However you like to spend your holidays, Algarve offers something for everybody. If you like lively resorts or quiet resorts, you'll find them but, best of all, with the help of this book, you can easily escape the crowds. Step out with us and share our delight at finding tranquillity and undreamed-of countryside — in the very heart of Algarve.

Acknowledgements

First and foremost we would like to thank the Portuguese National Tourist Office in London, and especially Pilar Pereira, for considerable help and support in making this book possible. Sincere thanks also to the following:

Isabel Oliveira, of the Região de Tourismo do Algarve, for her guidance; botanists Graça Silva and Armando Moura, from the Parque Natural da Ria Formosa, for sharing so freely their love and knowledge of the native flora and for being such lovely people; the Instituto Geográfico e Cadastral, Lisbon, for permitting us to adapt their topographical maps; Richard Wylie, of Dazer UK, who kindly supplied us with 'dog dazers', a most effective and very useful ultrasonic dog deterrent (see page 51); last but not least, thanks to our publishers Pat Underwood and John Seccombe for their constant faith and support.

Background reading

Algarve attracts no more than a small section in the general travel books on Portugal. Mostly these cover the same ground, and it is only necessary to read a small selection to absorb some background. The following have fairly good sections: Fodor's Portugal, Cadogan's Guide to Portugal and the Rough Guide to Portugal. For a broader picture, two books worth reading are the Insight Guide to Portugal and the Michelin Guide to Portugal and Madeira. To help with catering, a useful book is Carol Wright's 'Self-Catering in Portugal' (Croom Helm, 1986).

❋ Getting about

With so much interest focused on the coastal zone, it is not surprising to find this region is well served by public transport. **Buses** ply back and forth along the main highway, the EN125, calling in at the various coastal towns. There are two main bus companies. The buses that are mostly seen, especially east of Portimão, are those in orange livery — the RN buses, operated by Rodoviaria Nacional. The grey/blue buses of Castelo & Cacorino (C&C) operate routes to the western end of Algarve — you may use one to visit Monchique, for example. All the services are timetabled and generally keep good time. It always pays to arrive a few minutes earlier for the bus than the scheduled time. A selection of useful timetables for both companies is given in the timetable section, pages 129-133. Apart from the normal local bus services, the RN operates some **long-distance express** services, which can sometimes be useful for travelling in Algarve. They stop only at major centres. The Faro/Porto express, for example, calls at Vilamoura and Albufeira before heading north. The buses are generally much faster than the trains.

There is a very useful **train service** which runs almost the length of Algarve, from Lagos in the west to Vila Real on the eastern border. With 45 stations along this line, it can be a slow journey — taking as long as four and one-half hours to travel the whole length. But it is a fun way to travel and much cheaper than the buses. The full timetable is too long and detailed to include in the timetable section, but a short extract is given, which might be useful for getting to the start of some of the walks. Full timetables are available free of charge from most stations and some tourist information offices.

Taxis are plentiful in the main tourist resorts, and these are especially useful for getting out to some of the outlying regions. Meters are not commonly in use, so it is wise to enquire about the fare before you start the journey. In our limited experience, we found that the taxi drivers were fairly consistent in applying the fares, and that we were paying the same rates as the local people. If you can team up with other walkers to reduce the cost, then taxis represent a very convenient way of getting out into the countryside from the main centres but, in most cases, you would need to arrange to be collected to get back again.

The limitations of the public transport system are only fully realised when you want to get out and about into the inland villages and countryside — which you will need to do for many of our walks. This is where a hire car is invaluable. Car hire is relatively cheap in Algarve, much cheaper than in the rest of Portugal, and very popular. See the notes on pages 17-19 about car hire and driving.

COUNTRY FAIRS AND MARKETS

Market day is a day of great atmosphere and excitement for the local people. It is a chance to look for bargains, shop for locally-grown produce, buy goods that are not normally available in the local shops, or even sell or buy some livestock. Just about everything is on offer at some of the larger markets, and it is particularly those with a livestock section that are best described as 'country fairs'. Here temporary bars and eating places are set up, where the menfolk seal most of their bargains.

None of this is window-dressing for tourism, so here is an opportunity to see at first hand the ordinary life of the local people, to observe and appreciate their customs. It is a snapshot on life. You might also be tempted to buy; some of the home-produced honey is good value, as is bedding and towelling. If you feel like a snack while you are walking around, try the *filhos*, which look like doughnut rings — but make sure they are hot.

The markets are conveniently held on a regular timetable, most monthly.

Weekly markets

Saturdays: Loulé, São Bras   Every Wednesday: Quarteira

Fortnightly markets

Tuesdays (1st and 3rd in the month): Albufeira

Monthly markets

1st Sunday: Moncarapacho	1st Monday: Portimão
1st Friday: Sagres	1st Saturday: Lagos
2nd Sunday: Estói*	2nd Monday: Algoz*
3rd Monday: Silves	3rd Thursday: Alte
4th Saturday: Tunes	4th Monday: Messines

*These are two of the bigger markets — really country fairs

A country code for walkers and motorists

The experienced rambler is used to following a 'country code', but the tourist out for a lark may unwittingly cause damage, harm animals, and even endanger his own life. Do heed this advice:

- **Do not light fires**; everything gets tinder dry in summer. Stub out cigarettes with care.
- **Do not frighten animals**. The goats and sheep you may encounter on your walks are not tame. By making loud noises or trying to touch them or photograph them, you may cause them to run in fear and be hurt.
- **Walk quietly** through all farms, hamlets and villages, leaving all gates just as you found them. Gates do have a purpose, usually to keep animals in — or out of — an area. Remember, too, that a gate may be of a temporary nature — brushwood across the path — but it serves exactly the same purpose, so please replace it after passing.

Cork oak

- **Protect all wild and cultivated plants**. Don't try to pick wild flowers or uproot saplings. They will die before you even get back to the hotel. When photographing wild flowers, watch where you put your feet so that you do not destroy others in the process. Obviously fruit and crops are someone's private property and should not be touched.
- **Never walk over cultivated land.**
- **Take all your litter away with you.**
- **Walkers — do not take risks.** Do not attempt walks beyond your capacity and **never** walk alone. *Always* tell a responsible person — perhaps your hotel porter — exactly where you are going and what time you plan to return. Remember, if you become lost or injure yourself, it may be a long time before you are found. On any but a very short walk near to villages, it's a good idea to take along a torch, a whistle, a compass, extra water and warm clothing — as well as some high energy food like chocolate. Review the 'Important note to the reader' on page 2 and the 'Walkers' checklist' on page 54.

FARO — KEY

1 Tourist information
2 Main square
3 Police
4 TAP offices
5 Port
6 Marina
7 Telephones
8 Bank area
9 Museums
10 Bus station

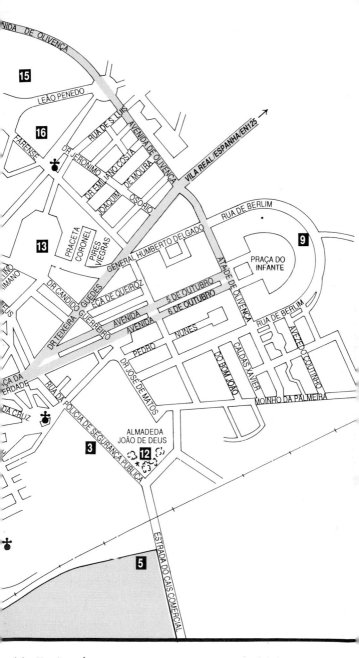

11 Taxi rank	17 Cathedral (old town)
12 Parks	18 Post offices
13 Market	19 Railway station
14 Customs	20 WC
15 Hospital	21 Water tower (near
16 Stadium	the road to São Bras)

11

✿ Picnicking

Beaches are popular venues for picnics in Algarve, but there are many lovely and more tranquil country locations. It is not unusual to find small picnic areas as you drive around. These are usually sited amongst trees, with wooden or stone tables and benches.

We have chosen a selection of picnic settings — some along the routes of our walks, others reached during the car tours. Some lie deep in the countryside, others on secluded beaches (but remember that in mid- summer *all* beaches are fairly busy). Most of these picnic spots are easily accessible on foot or by public/private transport. A few, due to their isolation, require more walking — but they are well worth the extra effort involved.

All the information you need to get to these picnic spots is given on the following pages, where *picnic numbers correspond to walk numbers* (the picnics on page 16, prefixed 'CT', are only accessible from the car tours). You can quickly find the general location of the picnic place by looking at the large touring map (on which the area of each walk is outlined in white). We include transport details (🚐 = how to get there by bus; 🚗 = where to leave your private transport), how long a walk you'll have, and views or setting. Beside the picnic title you'll find a map reference; the exact location of the picnic spot is shown on this *walking* map by the symbol *P* (the best place to leave a car will be indicated, too, by the symbol 🚗). Finally, to help you choose an appealing location, photograph references are given for each picnic suggestion, wherever possible.

Please remember that if more than a few minutes' walking is required, you will need to wear **sensible shoes** and to take a **sunhat** (o indicates a picnic **in full sun**). A plastic groundsheet or large plastic bags could be useful, especially early in the season when the ground might still be damp.

If you are travelling to your picnic by bus, refer to the timetables on pages 129-133, but remember — it's always a good idea to get up-to-date timetable information from the bus station or tourist information office.

If you are travelling to your picnic by hired transport, be extra vigilant off the main roads; children, animals and adults are often in the village streets. Be careful where you park: don't damage the vegetation and flowers, and be sure not to block a road or track.

Picnic food suggestions are not much of a problem in Algarve, where there are well-stocked modern supermarkets. Portimão, Albufeira, Faro and Olhão also boast large supermarkets with their own bakeries and butchers, where you can buy fresh bread, even on a Sunday. Locate the local bakery for a wide choice of fresh bread: *pão seco* (small bread rolls) are ideal for picnics. From the local market buy fresh *pepino* (cucumber), *tomates* (tomatoes), *alface* (lettuce), *pimentos* (peppers), *azeitonas* (olives: *verdes* = green, *pretas* = black), *iogurte* (yogurt), *mel* (honey), *queijo fresco* (very mild fresh goat's cheese), and a variety of fresh fruit depending on the season. Cheese slices and portions are readily available, but there is a limited selection of cheese. Cheese is rather a luxury item in Portugal and therefore expensive.

Portuguese specialities, which can be bought ready-made from the delicatessen counter, include *rissois* (rissoles) and croquettes. There is a choice of cooked meats and sausages. *Carne* = meat, usually *porco* (pork) or *carneiro* (lamb). *Peru* (turkey) and *frango* (chicken) are also popular. We also discovered small tins of sardine paté, ideal for picnics ... but be careful not to buy the 'piquant' variety, unless you like it hot. There is a varied selection of *bolos* (cakes), since cake and coffee play an important part in everyday Portuguese life. Food signs are not usually in English, so it helps to have a phrase book handy.

Last, but not least, don't forget something to drink. There is a wide range of soft drinks including fruit juice, flavoured yogurt drinks, and bottled water. For more heady refreshment, take a bottle of *vinho* (wine). Portugal offers a wide range of wines, and an enjoyable element of your holiday will probably be trying many of them. *Vinho verde* ('green wine', but usually white and slightly sparkling) is an excellent choice for picnics, but a rosé or light fruity red would be equally acceptable. *Saude!*

---

1 LUZ — OBELISK (Map page 58) ○

🚗 by car or taxi: 20min on foot . Park in the car park at Praia da Luz and follow the notes for Walk 1.

🚌 by bus: 25min on foot. Bus from Lagos to Luz (Timetable 1); alight in the main square. Follow the notes for Walk 2 (in reverse) from the 5min-point to get to Praia da Luz; then pick up and follow Walk 1.

It is a steep but short climb to this good vantage point offering excellent views, but no shade.

3a PONTA DA ALMADENA (map page 62) ○

🚗 by car or taxi: no walking. Park in the car park at Ponta da Almadena behind the café/bar, at the back of the inlet on the left, 2km along the road west from Burgau.

🚌 by bus: 35min on foot. Bus from Lagos to Burgau (Timetable 1); then follow the notes for Walk 3.

Large expanse of sandy beach, round to the left at the mouth of the inlet, beneath the cliffs. Little shade. Childrens' sandy play area in front of the café/bar.

3b ISOLATED FORT (map page 62; photograph page 65) ○

🚗 by car or taxi: 15min on foot. Park as in 3a above, then follow the notes for Walk 3 from the 35min-point.

🚌 by bus: 50min on foot. Bus as for 3a above, then follow the notes for Walk 3 to the 50min-point.

A secluded spot on the edge of the cliffs. Some shade from the fort walls.

3c BOCA DO RIO (Map page 62; photograph page 65) ○

🚗 by car or taxi: 27min on foot. Park as for 3a above, then follow the notes for Walk 3 from the 35min-point. Alternatively, park in the centre of Salema and follow the notes for Walk 3 in reverse to Boca do Rio.

🚌 by bus: 27min on foot. Bus from Lagos to Salema (Timetable 2), then follow the notes for Walk 3 in reverse.

A more stony but secluded beach, with the added interest of Roman remains and ancient salt pans. No shade.

5 RUINED CONVENT AT MONCHIQUE (map page 73)

🚗 by car or taxi: 11min on foot. Park in or near the main square at Monchique and follow the notes for Walk 5 as far as the convent.

🚌 by bus: 11min on foot. Bus from Portimão to Monchique (Timetable 3); then follow Walk 5.

A beautiful viewpoint overlooking Monchique, in a woodland setting of cork oaks and eucalyptus trees.

7a CALDAS DE MONCHIQUE (map page 73; photograph page 36)

🚗 by car or taxi: no walking. Park in the car park in Caldas. See the notes for Walk 7.

🚌 by bus: no walking. Bus from Portimão to Caldas de Monchique (Timetable 3); alight in the centre of Caldas, by the car park. See the notes for Walk 7.

Pleasant shaded areas where you can enjoy the ambience of this ancient spa.

7b SHADED RIVERSIDE (map page 73; photograph page 77)

🚗 by car or taxi: up to 5min on foot. Either park in the car park at Caldas de Monchique and follow the notes for Walk 7 (5min), or continue round through Caldas to park by the roadside near the bottling plant at the end of the one-way system (see the notes for Walk 7, at the 5min-point).

🚌 by bus: up to 5min on foot. Bus from Portimão to Caldas de Monchique (Timetable 3); alight in Caldas centre, or stay on the bus as far as the bottling plant on the way out. Follow the notes for Walk 7 either from the start or from the 5min-point.

A tranquil area by the river, where sunlight filtering through the trees creates dappled patterns.

9 SILVES WINDMILL (map page 81; photograph page 82) ○

🚗 by car or taxi: 32min on foot. Park in the large car park by the river below the town and follow the notes for Walk 9.
🚌 by bus: 32min on foot. Bus from Portimão to Silves (Timetables 4, 5 and 11), then follow the notes for Walk 9.
A wonderful panoramic location, carpeted with flowers in springtime.

10a MARINHA (map page 85; cover photograph and page 86) ○

🚗 only accessible by car or taxi: 4min on foot. To reach Marinha, turn south off the EN125 opposite the International School, heading towards Benagil. (This school is located 3km east of the Lagoa roundabout and 2km west of Porches.) Some 4km down this road, turn left at the road signposted 'Praia da Marinha'. Park in car park on clifftop above the beach and follow Walk 10 from the 26min-point.
Breathtaking — a magnificent beach! Very natural, with limited facilities and little shade.

10b PRAIA DE ALBANDEIRA (map page 85) ○

🚗 only accessible by car or taxi: up to 22min on foot. To reach Praia de Albandeira, turn south towards Benagil opposite the International School (see 10a). After 3km, turn left onto the track signposted 'Praia de Albandeira' and prepare yourself for a bumpy ride down a narrow track for a few kilometres. Park behind the beach (no walking). Alternatively, park as for 10a and follow Walk 10 from the 26min-point (22min).
An out-of-the-way spot with limited facilities and no shade.

12 ALTE FOUNTAIN (map page 95; photograph page 93)

🚗 only accessible by car or taxi: no walking. Park at the picnic site, by following the notes for Car Tour 3 on pages 37 and 38.
An official picnic site by the river where trees provide ample shade. Full facilities available.

13 PADERNE CASTLE (map page 98; photograph page 97)

🚗 by car or taxi: 32min on foot. Park on the main road near the road signposted 'Fonte' and follow Walk 13 from the 3min-point.
🚌 by bus: 35min on foot. Bus from Albufeira to Paderne (Timetable 7), then follow the notes for Walk 13.
Lovely viewpoint from an old Moorish castle set in the heart of the countryside.

14 ROCHA DA PENA (map page 102; photograph page 101)

🚗 only accessible by car or taxi: 29min on foot. Park as for Walk 14 and follow the walking notes as far as the 29min-point.
Picnic under the carob trees and enjoy extensive views out over the farmland below.

15 SALIR (map page 103; photograph page 32)

🚗 only accessible by car or taxi: 5min on foot. Park on the wide road below the village, as in Car Tour 3, then head up towards the church and water tower. Read Walk 15, from the 2h-point, to visit the castle.
Extensive, superb panorama from this strategic viewpoint.

17 RUINED WATERMILL (map page 117) ○

🚗 by car or taxi: 12min on foot. Follow the 'Sanatório' signs from São Bras. Tareja is on the left, further along the road past the sanatorium entrance. Park near the track off left just past Tareja, before the surfaced road ends (there is a fountain below left). Walk down the track to the left (with a stream below on your right), following the notes for Walk 17 (Short walk 2, but in reverse, from the 1h02min-point). Pick up the notes for the main walk (53min-point) and follow them to the river (2min).

🚌 by bus: 50min on foot. Bus from Faro to São Bras (Timetable 6). Follow the notes for Walk 17 as far as the 35min-point, where you turn right along the surfaced road to reach the track and fountain on the left in 39min. Turn left down the track and follow the notes for motorists above.

A tranquil and secluded riverside setting by a ruined water-mill. If you have children with you keep them out of the water-mill which has a small but uncovered deep hole inside, possibly a well. The photograph on page 114 was taken nearby.

20 CASTRO MARIM (map page 125; photograph pages 32-33) ○

🚗 only accessible by car or taxi: 3min on foot. See Car Tour 4 (page 44) for details of how to get there and park.
Sheltered picnic area within the castle grounds.

CT1 BARRAGEM DA BRAVURA (see the touring map) ○

🚗 only accessible by car or taxi: no walking. Park in the car park by the restaurant at the dam (*barragem*), reached by following the notes for Car Tour 1 as far as the 24km-point at Odiaxere (page 21) and turning right in the centre. The narrow surfaced road leads in 9km to the dam. Just before descending to the car park, there is another car parking area on the left, which is a good viewpoint. This is also a marvellous area in spring for a variety of wild flowers.
Situated amongst the rolling matos-covered hills with a view of the Serra de Monchique.

CT2 BARRAGEM DO ARADE (see the touring map) ○

🚗 only accessible by car or taxi: no walking. Park in the car park to the left as you arrive at the dam (*barragem*). The surfaced road to the dam is on the right, 10km from São Bartolomeu de Messines in the direction of Silves, or on the left 7km from Silves (Car tour 2, page 27). It is then a further 3.5km down this road to the *barragem*.
On the edge of the matos-covered hills, so typical of inland Algarve, this dam has the added interest of an island which can be visited by boat. Facilities include a restaurant/café with sun bathing terrace and boat hire.

CT3a FONTE DE BENÉMOLA (see the touring map) ○

🚗 only accessible by car or taxi: 20min on foot. See Circular walk for motorists on pages 34-35 for details on how to get there and park.
A river location hidden in the depths of pastoral countryside.

CT3b BARREIRAS BRANCAS (see the touring map; photograph page 27) ○

🚗 only accessible by car or taxi: 20min on foot. See Circular walk for motorists, page 41, for details on how to get there and park.
Share this lovely vantage point with an old windmill.

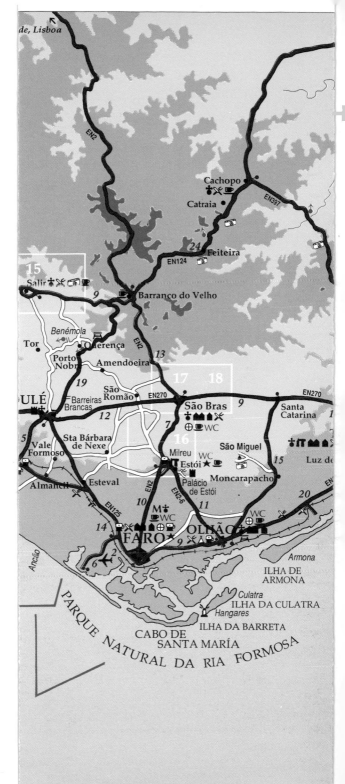

some unspoken agreement that they aren't necessary in built-up areas. Always wear your seat belt!

Petrol stations are fairly frequent along the EN125, and many of them are open seven days a week; some of the international companies offer a 24 hour service. There are few petrol stations in country areas, and many are closed on Sunday. If you are heading inland, go with a full tank of petrol. Some grades of petrol may be unfamiliar: *super* is self-explanatory, but *gasoleo* = diesel and *sem chumbo* = unleaded (only available from the major international companies). Water fountains can be found by roadsides throughout the countryside. *Agua* = water; *agua potavel* = drinking water.

Drive carefully: the road is regarded as a pavement, especially in country areas. Be extra vigilant for animals and the large-wheeled carts often encountered in the country. Be aware also that even main roads almost invariably narrow appreciably where they cross bridges and sometimes where they pass through small villages; there are usually no warnings. Indeed, a general lack of road signs and road markings can be disconcerting at times, so take extra care.

The general standard of driving lacks the discipline to which we are accustomed — particularly with regard to overtaking. The EN125 along the coast is treated as a motorway by the locals. It is mainly a single-lane flow, with an additional lane at the side for breakdowns and very slow moving traffic like farm tractors. But it is the habit of some drivers to overtake, when there's no room to do so, knowing that they can force the on-coming traffic into the slow lane. In some places there are short, well-signposted stretches, expressly for overtaking. Another common occurrence is for a driver to suddenly stop and chat to friends by the roadside or in a passing vehicle, even if he's in the middle of a stream of traffic. The significance of zebra crossings is confusing, as there are no beacons to indicate their presence. Roadworks are not always indicated well in advance, especially those that reduce traffic flow. There are frequent police checks, so make sure you have the relevant documents relating to your vehicle, your driving licence and passport to hand.

Remember to take a pocket phrase book if only for the road signs; you won't find them written in English. A parking sign depicting what looks like a comb and a car = park at an angle to the road to maximise parking space; *perigo* = danger; *desvio* = diversion; *lombas* = a ridge in the road to slow traffic. (The intriguing 'Património do Estado' engraved on many buildings and monuments simply translates to 'government property'.)

Telephones are located in or near post offices; otherwise hotels, restaurants, bars and shops will let you use their phones (but their per unit rates may be unreasonably high). **WCs** are available in most towns, almost always in market halls; others are found in bus and railway stations, restaurants, cafés and some petrol stations. Don't always rely on toilet paper being supplied, carry your own.

The **touring notes** are brief: they include little history or information about the towns. Some literature is available from tourist offices, and sometimes we refer you to the walking notes for more comment but, for more information, see our background reading list on page 6. We concentrate mainly on the 'logistics' of touring: times and distances, road conditions, viewpoints and good places to rest. Most of all we emphasise possibilities for **walking** and **picnicking**; for information about the picnic spots highlighted in the notes, see pages 12-16. If you want to stretch your legs, look at the short walks listed with the main walks. This should give you a taste of the landscapes, sufficient to whet your appetite for more.

There are many centres of tourism along the coast of Algarve, all of which can easily be keyed into the routes of the car tours from our chosen starting points. Two of the tours start in the east, from Faro, and two in the west, from the Lagoa roundabout on the EN125.

Allow plenty of time for **stops:** our times include only short breaks at viewpoints labelled (🕿) in the touring notes. Distances quoted are *cumulative km* from Faro or the Lagoa roundabout. A key to the symbols in the notes is on the touring map.

If you only hire a car for one day, Tour 1, a long trip, provides a sampler encompassing the windswept coast and the pastoral serenity of the Serra de Monchique. If you don't wish to drive quite as far, Tour 3 takes you through an appealing and gentler countryside, punctuated by the intriguing Rochas of Pena and Soidos. Most of our hire cars recorded whole kilometres only, so our distances are not always accurate to the nearest decimal point, which left us guessing a little at some distances below a kilometre. This shouldn't cause any problems when used in conjunction with the other instructions.

All motorists should read the country code on page 9 and go quietly in the countryside.

1 THE WEST COAST TOUR

Lagoa • (Portimão) • Lagos • Sagres • Aljezur • Marmelete • Silves • Lagoa

189.5km/117.5mi; about 3 hours 30minutes' driving: start from the Lagoa roundabout, on the EN125, heading west towards Portimão.

On route: Picnics (see pages 12-16) 1, 3a-c, 7a, 7b, 9, (10a, 10b), also at the Barragem de Bravura and the Barragem do Arade; Walks 1–9, (10)

Variable road surfaces call for constant vigilance on the part of the driver. Even when the road surface is new, subsidence can still be a problem, and it is not unusual to encounter sunken areas with no warning signs. The EN125 is well surfaced and good on the whole, but negotiating the area around Portimão, where extensive road- and bridge-building is in progress, is best avoided at peak times (diversions are in operation which look set to continue for a year or two at least). West of Lagos the surface deteriorates, except for some stretches between Sagres and Cape St Vincent, Aljezur to Marmelete and Nave to Silves. There were some notable areas of unmarked subsidence between Aljezur and Marmelete. The road between Silves and Lagoa was in sore need of resurfacing when we were there.

Visit the pleasant resort of Lagos and enjoy a spectacular coastline which still harbours a few relatively unspoilt fishing villages. Windswept Sagres, one time home of Prince Henry the Navigator, is now a favoured spot for fishermen who hang precariously from the rocky cliffs at dizzy heights, casting their lines into the waves below. Follow the Atlantic coastline northwards, past deserted sandy beaches. Visit the castle at Aljezur, before turning inland to yet more dramatic scenery, as you head towards the highest mountain range in Algarve.

Starting from the roundabout at **Lagoa** on the EN125, head west towards Portimão. Almost immediately there is a left turn to a 'water slide' park, but keep ahead on the main road. Continue until you reach a crossroads and traffic lights (6km). Normally you can drive straight ahead to Portimão, but at the time of writing you have to turn right here and follow a diversion. This takes you through the village of Mexilhoeira da Carregação, then back onto the EN125. Until the new bridge and attendant road-building is complete, you can expect diversions and hold-ups around Portimão.

Cross the narrow road bridge (9.8km) and turn left if you wish to visit Portimão (▲▲▲✕☎⊕⚓WC), but keep straight ahead otherwise. If you stop in Portimão, return to the bridge and turn left to continue — adding just 1km to the overall total. At the point where the road starts to bend round to the right in the direction of Monchique (11km), fork left to Lagos. It is difficult to tell who has right of way here, so err on the side of caution. At the junction just afterwards, turn right onto the road which will take you directly to Lagos. Notice the road off left to Praia da Rocha (12.2km ⛰️⛰️🏠✕⛱️): this is a possible return route back through Portimão (follow the 'Faro' signs) for those who may wish to shorten the car tour by returning from Sagres or the intermediate villages along the same route.

The next major junction is a left turn to Alvor (13.7km), but our route continues ahead through pleasant country-side. At **Odiáxere** (24km) the road narrows to pass between the houses. In the centre of the village, you could turn right to the Barragem da Bravura (Picnic CT1). The bridge crossing the Ribeira de Bensafrim on the approach to Lagos is swiftly reached and the town itself can be seen, shimmering white, on the far shore. Immediately over the bridge is the Lagos roundabout. The main route is straight ahead, but first we make a short diversion into **Lagos**★ (28.2km ⛽🚻⛰️⛰️🏠✕🖼️△⛱️MWC) by turning left. Continue alongside the river for 1.3km, where you will find car parks and plenty of parking on the roadside.

Return to the roundabout and turn left to continue. Following the signs to Sagres, keep ahead through traffic lights and turn right at the T-junction (29.6km). (A left turn leads to Ponta da Piedade (photograph pages 58-9), Porto de Mós and Praia Dona Ana — all visited on the route of Walk 1.) If you can raise your eyes from the now-poor road surface, the pretty, gently undulating countryside is very appealing. Pass the turn off to Luz (🚻⛰️⛰️🏠✕△⛱️WC; Walks 1 and 2; Picnic 1) in 31.5km — the village is 3.1km down the road to the left. Once past **Espiche**, after 39.5km, notice the left turn to Burgau★ (🏠✕⛱️WC; Walk 3 and Picnics 3a-c). Burgau, shown on page 30, is 2km down the road, and Ponta da Almadena (Picnic 3a) a further 2km west from there. *Matos*-covered rolling hills with pockets of cultivation lie beyond the tree-lined road. This soon takes on a wilder aspect once you pass **Vale de Boi** (42.5km). Soon after **Budens** (43.5km 🚻) there is a left turn to Salema★ (44.5km ⛰️⛰️🏠✕⛱️WC; Walk 3; Picnic 3c), 2km down the road.

There are fewer signs of habitation here, as the *matos*, now becoming stunted in growth due to the windswept location, invades the countryside. At 47.5km there are some picnic tables under the trees to the left, and the road becomes quite bumpy before **Raposeira** (50.5km). Large tracts of pastureland dominate the scenery, where few trees dot the landscape. This gives way to green and well-farmed, gently-rolling hills as you approach **Vila do Bispo**

(52.5km ✚✗), where the main road keeps round left to Sagres. An obvious absence of trees, except for those lining the road, announces the windswept and wild nature of this narrow strip of land jutting out into the Atlantic.

The imposing frontage of the fort (Fortaleza de Sagres) fills in the landscape as you approach the roundabout (61.5km). Keep ahead to visit it (62.5km). It is possible to drive into the fort, but this could cause problems when it is busy in summer, since the entrance is a tunnel only wide enough for one car. Alternatively, park in the large car park outside. Inside, there is a huge pebble wind-compass (*rosa dos ventos*), a chapel, a tourist office and a youth hostel. You can also walk out to Sagres lighthouse at the end of the promontory (📷) and watch the local men fishing from precarious perches overhanging the sea far below. Return to the roundabout and turn right into **Sagres** ★ (🏔🔺✗� 🚎). Almost immediately there is a square on the right which is a pleasant café area, from where it is about 1km further down to the fishing harbour.

Head back to the roundabout to continue towards Cape St Vincent on a much-improved road; it heads straight through low scrub towards the lighthouse at the cape. Although the elements may have tried to subdue growth in this corner of Algarve, the botanist may well be surprised at the variety of flora awaiting discovery amongst the cowering bushes. Just before reaching the lighthouse, there is another fort on the right, the Fortaleza de Beliche (70.5km ✗). **Cabo de São Vicente** (Cape St Vincent) is reached in 71.5km. The lighthouse grounds are open to the public, and its position 9 degrees west of Greenwich makes it one of the most westerly points in Europe. From this viewpoint the Sagres lighthouse and the dark, forbidding bulk of the fort can be clearly seen. One word of caution. If a gale is blowing in the rest of Algarve, save your visit for another day, as this area is windswept at the best of times.

Retrace your route back to the far side of **Vila do Bispo** (87.5km ✗) and turn left (signposted for Aljezur and Lisbon). This junction is easy to miss, as Vila do Bispo is only a hamlet. The tree-lined road now runs parallel with the coast through softer, more undulating terrain. From **Carrapateira** (101.5km 🚎), an isolated spot, three tracks fairly close together lead off left to mainly-deserted sandy beaches. Pockets of green cultivation make patterns among the *matos*-covered low hills. Just as you notice a slight improvement in the road surface, you meet a patch of subsidence at **Bordeira** (105.5km). Golden yellow fields of lupins catch the eye in spring as the road winds uphill, past a lay-by on the left (109.5km), to meet the main Lagos/Lisbon road (EN120; 115.5km). Keep ahead on joining this main road (you may notice a few windmills dotting the landscape), and pass another lay-by on the right in 118.5km.

As you approach Aljezur you will see the castle on the hill above the town. Drive through **Aljezur** (121.5km ▮▲✕🍴🛏🚗 🚻WC), where the main road sweeps round right and over a bridge. Park on the left, just over the bridge, by the tourist office. To walk up to the castle (ten minutes), cross back over the river on a footbridge, to a small square. With your back towards the river, take the cobbled road up from the far right-hand corner of the square and continue round to the left, to climb through old Aljezur. When you meet a track, turn left up to the castle. Nothing much remains of it besides the walls, which look impressive from below, a vaulted cistern and two towers. The castle provides an excellent viewpoint, however: looking inland Foia, the highest peak in Algarve and the setting for Walk 5, can be spotted in the distance.

Leave the car park and turn left towards Lisbon; almost immediately there is a junction, where you go right towards Marmelete and Monchique. In less than 2km from Aljezur we found the bridge over the river had been destroyed by flood waters. A diversion to the right along a track and over a concrete bridge circumvented this obstacle, and we were soon back on the road. This is a spectacular run along a high-level road (📷) which wends ever upwards, crossing a narrow ridge where valleys plunge down steeply on either side. Pretty hollows of cultivation and the rolling *matos*-covered hills which become a carpet of white flowers in spring catch the eye (📷). The road surface is new, but there are stretches of bad subsidence, usually unmarked, so continue to be vigilant.

As you start to descend (134km) there are glimpses of the Barragem da Bravura not too far to the right (📷). Foia, the highest point, distinguished by its attendant cluster of antennae, can also be seen ahead. On reaching **Marmelete** (137.5km ☂), the new surface ends on meeting a narrower and rougher old road. Woodland now softens and cloaks the landscape, as the left turn to Chilrão (143.5km; Walk 4) is passed. On the approach to **Casais** (146.5km) the trees screening the roadside part to reveal views to the right over the countryside. Suddenly, as you penetrate further into the Serra de Monchique, the scene changes yet again, as deep terraced valleys create an interesting alpine picture (⌖). Foia (Walk 5) lies up to the left and, in 150.3km, you pass the point where Walk 6 crosses the road (about 200m before the Monchique/Portimão road junction).

Turn right down towards Portimão on reaching the main road (150.5km). A left turn would take you up to Monchique★ (♦▲▲✕♨⊕⚌WC ; Walks 4, 5, 6, 8; Picnic 5). See Car Tour 2 for more details about Monchique. In 3km pass the 'Miradouro das Caldas' (⌖) on the right, which is a good viewpoint over Caldas de Monchique. (The track for Walk 7 goes off right on the corner, just before reaching the viewpoint.) Continue to wind downhill on a good surfaced road and, if you have time to visit Caldas★ (▲▲▲✕♨🅿⚌WC; Car tour 2; Walks and Picnics 7a and 7b), turn right in a further 1.3km. This right turn, the only vehicular access into the centre of Caldas, is difficult from this approach, as it is an acute-angled turn back the way you came. Pass the next right turn, the exit from the one-way system through Caldas, in 156.2km; this is also an access point for the thermal hospital and the spa water bottling plant, so it is possible to turn right here and park at the end of the one-way system, if you are planning to enjoy Walk 7 or Picnic 7b. Continuing downhill, there is a large shaded lay-by on the left (157.4km), where one can park well away from the road. Once down from the hills (160.9km), the wooded areas are left behind, and the road straightens out as it heads towards Portimão.

Turn left to Silves at **Porto de Lagos**, in 167km, but keep straight on for Portimão and Lagos. Although the distance to Lagoa is shorter via Portimão than via Silves, until the new bridge and road by-passing Portimão is completed, it is best to avoid that route. Enjoy some tranquil scenery as you drive along this well-surfaced but winding road to **Silves**★ (177.9km ♦️🛉🏠▲✕♨⊕🅿M⚌WC; Walk 9; Picnics 9 and CT2). If you wish to stop at Silves, which is up on the left, park in one of the parking areas alongside the road skirting the town. The parking areas nearer the old bridge are more convenient for the historical centre. See Walk 9 for more details, and photograph page 82.

Continue back to Lagoa by turning right over the river below Silves (179.3km), and then turn right again. Hopefully, the road surface between Silves and Lagoa will be much improved when you use this book, but it was in a poor state of repair when we were last there. Pass Silves railway station (180.9km; you may have to stop here for the level crossing) and soon find yourselves on the outskirts of Lagoa. Look carefully for and take the left fork, signposted to Faro. Skirt round Lagoa following the Faro signs back to the EN125, and then turn right back to the **Lagoa roundabout** (186.8km). This is easier than trying to negotiate the narrow centre of Lagoa if it is busy.

Unknown Algarve: these gloriously green rolling hills lie between Tavira and Cachopo (Car tour 4). See also pages 31 and 34-35.

2 MOUNTAINS AND 'MOORS'

Lagoa • Silves • Caldas de Monchique • Monchique • Foia • Lagoa

91km/57mi; about 2 hours' driving: start from Lagoa roundabout, on main EN125 road, and head north to Silves.

On route: Picnics (see pages 12-16) 5, 7a, 7b, 9, also at the Barragem do Arade; Walks 4-9, (10)

From Lagoa the road is in a poor state of repair until you reach Silves, but there is a dramatic improvement from Silves up to Monchique. The road up from Monchique to Foia is narrow, but wide enough for two cars. It is also patchy in parts, especially close to Monchique and nearer the top. If possible, save this tour for a day when you can see the Serra de Monchique clearly from Lagoa, so that you will be able fully to appreciate the superb views.

Highlights on this memorable tour include the imposing remains at Silves — the Moors' capital of Algarve, an ancient spa set amidst soft green foliage and recalling days gone by, and the breathtaking views from the highest point in the tour, Foia.

From Lagoa (♨▲✕☎⏧) follow the signs inland to Silves. The road surface as far as Silves is in poor condition, which makes for a bumpy ride. Silves railway station is passed after 5.9km; then the road descends to the river below the town, providing a good vantage point (📷) for views of the castle at Silves★ (♨⛪▲✕☎⊕⌂⏧MWC;

Windmill near Albufeira

The splendid panorama from the mill at Barreiras Brancas (Car tour 3; Picnic CT3b).

Walk 9 and Picnic 9; photograph page 82). The castle ramparts glow red in early morning or evening sunlight. Turn left over the river and left again at the T-junction (7.5km), where there is a large car park and also parking along the roadside on the right. See the notes with Walk 9 for more information about Silves and to guide you up to the town centre. (A right turn at the T-junction leads in the direction of São Bartolomeu de Messines and the Barragem do Arade (Picnic CT2). This road passes the 'Cruz de Portugal', a 16th-century cross which is set on the left just past the next exit from Silves.) Besides the interesting historical remains and a small museum, the daily market in Silves, almost opposite the old bridge, is excellent for fresh produce.

Leave Silves and continue west in the direction of Monchique. The large exhibition centre, on the left as you leave Silves, features many events throughout the year, such as the orange festival in March; details can be obtained from tourist offices. A winding road now leads through pretty pastoral countryside, where oranges and lemons grow in abundance. This is a major orange-growing area, and you will pass many roadside stalls selling oranges en route to Monchique.

Meet a major T-junction after 18.4km and turn right towards Monchique and the mountains. A mass of purple from the many Judas trees lining the road here brings a splash of colour in spring. Enjoy a pleasant drive towards the foothills of the distinctive Serra de Monchique, past cultivated fields and through scattered hamlets. Fields

27

give way to woodland as the road starts to wind and twist uphill (24.5km). This is a beautiful climb on days when the sun filtering through the trees casts dancing, shimmering shadows. Pass a very large shady lay-by on the right (28km), before reaching the exit road from Caldas de Monchique on the left (29.2km). This is the entrance to the thermal hospital and the spa water bottling plant, but the exit for the one-way system through Caldas itself. It is possible to turn left here and park near the end of the one-way system for Walk 7 and Picnic 7b, leaving a five-minute walk into Caldas centre. To visit **Caldas ★ (▲▲ ▲ ✕ ☎ ♿ ⛉ wc;** Walks 6 and 7; Picnics 7a and 7b) by car, turn left at the next road (29.6km) and park in the centre car park (30km) or, if that's full, continue through and park by the roadside on the way out. Caldas (see photograph page 36) is well worth a visit just to enjoy its old world ambience. It became one of our favourite 'coffee stops'.

Leave Caldas by the one-way system and turn left to continue to wind up in the direction of Monchique, again passing the fork down left to Caldas (31km) a few moments later. A further 1.3km brings you to a superb viewpoint over Caldas on the left, the **Miradouro das Caldas** (32.3km ✕ ⛉ ⊚). Also on the left, at the next corner (32.6km), is the track down to Caldas followed in Walks 6 and 7. The path for the same walks enters from the left on 32.8km.

At **Nave** (34.6km) there is a turn left to Marmelete opposite a quarry on the right, but keep ahead for

Monchique. Just after a petrol station on the left, as you enter Monchique, come to a crossroads (36.6km). The road to the left will be your route up to Foia. (If you have time to spare, a right turn here leads via a surfaced road to Alferce (16km return; ⛩), a pretty run through woodland affording some excellent views (📷) across the valley to the left.) Keep straight on up to 5th October Square in **Monchique**★ (✝⛪✕🅿⊕☕WC; Walks 4, 5, 6, 8; Picnic 5), where you can park either in the square on the left or in a lay-by to the right. It is worthwhile trying the first part of Walk 5 as far as the convent. This guides you up through old Monchique to a good vantage point from where it's possible to enjoy views (📷) across the valley in the direction of Picota (Walk 8).

On leaving Monchique, return to the crossroads and turn right up to Foia (38km). Go left at the small roundabout soon encountered. The road now rises rapidly above Monchique, and the surface also improves. Fantastic views open out to the left (📷) as you wend your way up through forests of eucalyptus trees. As you reach the point where the vegetation starts to become more sparse and the road surface deteriorates a little (43.8km) there is a *fonte* and *miradouro* on the left; this is the starting point for Walk 4. The final 2km drive up to the summit, through mainly low lying heather and cistus, provides almost uninterrupted views (📷) over the countryside to the left. On the approach to **Foia** (✕📷☕), keep left to the car park. The summit is unfortunately home to a forest of televsion and radio masts, as well as a souvenir complex. But if you follow the notes for Walk 5 (Short walk 2) for about ten minutes, these will take you off the summit and to the fine views shown on pages 70-71).

Return then to the main road (54.2km) and turn right in the direction of Portimão, following your outward route back to **Lagoa**.

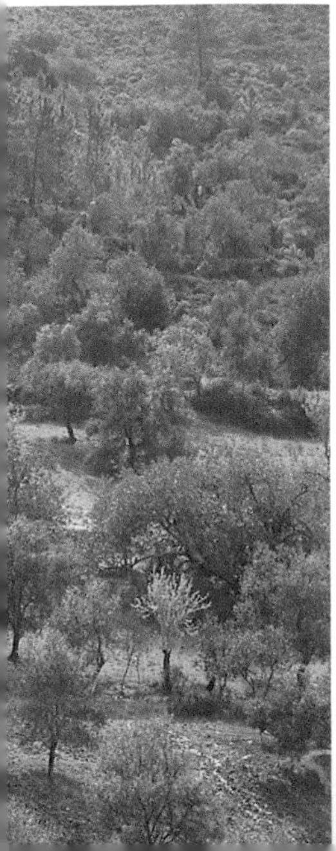

This lovely valley is encountered in Walk 11, which is also illustrated on pages 88 and 90. Car tour 3 passes close by, and you might like to make a diversion to visit the valley — it's on the route of Short walk 11-1.

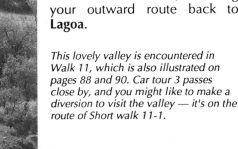

3 VILLAGES OF THE BARROCAL

**Faro • Estói • Bordeira • Amendoeira • Salir • Alte •
Paderne • Bouliqueime • Faro**

*106km/65.75mi; about 2 hours 20 minutes' driving: exit Faro from the
harbour (see town plan pages 10-11).*

On route: Picnics (see pages 12-16) 12-15, also at the Fonte de
Benemola and Barreiras Brancas; Walks 11-16

*On the whole, the country roads used on this tour are not too badly
surfaced, but you may still encounter a few potholes and bumpy
stretches, where the surface has been damaged. Petrol is not as readily
available inland as it is nearer the coast, so make sure you have enough
before setting out. Note that both Estói Palace and the Ruins of Milreu
are closed on Mondays.*

A pink palace, some Roman ruins, a Moorish castle,
gently-rolling pastoral countryside, and sleepy
inland villages weave a fascinating tapestry into the
central limestone region of Algarve — the Barrocal,
described on pages 89 and 90.

Faro has a confusing one-way system in its centre and,
unless you are familiar with the town (which can become
very congested), it is easier to keep to the peripheral roads.
You can start the tour in either of two ways. 1) Start from
the harbour, heading east towards the old town. Continue
around to the left, away from the seafront, passing the

*Burgau (Car tour 1
and Walk 2) is one
of the Algarvian
fishing villages that
has retained its
character despite
all the touristic
development
further east along
this splendid coast.*

Farmhouse on the road between Tavira and Cachopo; see also pages 25 and 34-35 for more photographs of this enchanting area (Car tour 1).

tourist office on the right, and then keep right in the one-way system. Go left to meet the Praça da Liberdade, where you turn right, and keep straight ahead into Avenida 5 de Outubro. Turn left at the roundabout at the top of the avenue into Ataide de Olivença. Keep on this road, following the hospital signs, until you come to the EN2 signposted to São Bras, where you turn right (2km), just before reaching a large yellow and white water tower, also on the right. Alternatively, follow the airport signs west out of Faro onto the EN125 and turn right, towards Spain and the hospital, at the ring road traffic lights. Turn left onto the EN2 signposted to São Bras, just beyond the yellow and white water tower on the left.

Whichever exit you choose, the EN2 leads you quickly out across the plain to the Algarvian foothills and to the right turn to Estói, reached after 10km. There are two right turns: ignore the first one, a fork to the right, but take the second one, at the crossroads shortly afterwards.

At the ruins of **Milreu** (10.2km **i**), turn left into the site, where you can park (see Walk 16 for more details about this interesting site with many excavated remains to be seen). Turn left on leaving Milreu and continue into **Estói★** (11.1km **i** **⬛** WC). Park in the square on the left. As you enter the main square, you can see the gates of the palace up to your left. The gates give access to the gardens, which are worth a visit for their curiosity value, but the palace itself is not open to the public. If you would like a closer look at the palace buildings, follow the notes for Walk 16 — in reverse — from Estói centre.

This narrow lane leads to the ramparts of the castle in the lovely village of Salir (Car tour 2, Picnic 15, Walk 15). A typical Algarvian chimney is also seen in the photograph.

Return by the same route back to the main road to São Bras, turning right immediately after crossing the bridge at the minor crossroads. Pass a petrol station on the left, just before meeting the main road, where you turn right (12.3km). Almost at once (12.4km), take the left turn signposted to Bordeira. A scenic route along winding country roads, through lovely rural countryside like that shown on pages 110-111, raises you gently into the rolling

Algarve offers good opportunities for bird watching. The nature reserve at Castro Marim is an ideal place for this, and Walk 20 tells you how to get into the heart of the reserve. This photograph was taken along that walk, and the castle itself (Picnic 20) is visible in the background.

Generally, the old salt pans or 'salinas', which can be found at various parts along the coast always have a high population of waders. The Parque Natural da Ria Formosa is good, too, for bird watching, and the authorities there plan to start, possibly during 1990, boat trips around the area of the sandbanks.

Other wetland areas of interest lie near the coast between Albufeira and Armação de Pêra, the whole of the river estuary from Lagos up to Silves, and an area near Salema mentioned in Walk 3.

Overleaf: the landscape near Cachopo (Car tour 4); see also pages 25 and 31.

hills (). Just after a sharp bend to the left, meet significant looking crossroads (19km) and keep ahead to the main Loulé/São Bras road (20km). Turn left, and be ready to turn right almost immediately (signposted 'São Romão' and 'Alportel'), back onto a country road. Rise up through **São Romão** and come to a division (21km), where you go left to Amendoeira. Striking deeper into the hinterland, the former rural aspect gives way to a more barren landscape. *Matos*, interspersed with pockets of cultivation, becomes more predominant as you near **Amendoeira** (24km). Reach the main Loulé/Barranco do Velho road and turn right (27km). Stay on this road for a short while, through **Porto Nobre** (28km), where pine trees lining the road give a more alpine feel to the surroundings. Fork off left towards 'Querença' and 'Tor' after 30km, and ignore a left turn to Querença shortly afterwards.

Keep along the road towards Tor, until you turn right to 'Alte' and 'Lisbon' in 32km. (Keep ahead here for a further 1km, if you wish to visit Fonte de Benémola — Picnic CT3a; see circular walk suggestion on the next page.) Here is yet another twisting road which wends its way through the undulating countryside, past almond groves like those in the photograph on page 105 and through hamlets (). Watch out for some sharp bends along this stretch, and also some badly-eroded sections of road. The route of Walk 15 joins in from the left after 37.1km and

→ **FONTE DE BENÉMOLA** 🚗 Circular walk for motorists →

Buried deep in the countryside is a little known beauty spot by a river, the Fonte de Benemola. It is just a short walk of about 3.5km/2.2mi, taking around 40min, to this beauty spot and back — or 55min, if you complete the whole circuit. If you are in the area, or if you want a break during Car tour 3, then try it as a short walk or for a picnic outing.

Follow the notes for Car tour 3 to the 32km-point, on the EN524, where you keep ahead towards Tor, instead of turning right. Look for a track on the right about 1km further on, signposted 'Fonte de Bené-mola'. Park off the road, by the abandoned house on the left, as you enter the track — or at a convenient place on the road.

Start walking down the track, which is unsuitable for cars, along the side of a shallow valley. The deep green foliage of the orange trees and the ordered cultivation down on the left contrasts sharply with the scrubland up to the right. It is this scrubland, however, which shelters a wealth of wild flowers, including *Astragalus lusitanicus*, with its creamy-yellow pea-like flowers, the cheerful yellow *Anemone palmata*, and a number of orchids. At a division in the track (**10min**),

keep down left. Head down towards a stream and the leafy shade of a natural beauty spot, where you cross a bridge over the stream. Turn left (**12min**), when the track divides beyond the bridge. Orange, lemon and carob trees cluster together on the left, the scent of the citrus flowers providing an added delight in spring. Keep left at the next division, in just under **14min**, staying ahead with the river on your left, to reach the Fonte and picnic area in **20min**. It is possible to explore further up stream where the river flows through a small ravine.

To make the walk circular, you can ford the river to the left just past the picnic site, and continue left again on the path downstream. Keep the river on your left and don't be tempted to wander away from it to the right. When you emerge by a bridge on the EN524, turn left to cross the bridge, and follow the road round left, back to where you parked, five minutes away. We couldn't complete the circuit ourselves, due to the river being in full flow, but we estimate that it would take about 35 minutes to return to the car by this route. Otherwise, return to where you parked by the same outward route.

Caldas de Monchique — a delightful old spa town and one of our favourite 'watering holes' (Picnic 7a, Walk 6, Car tour 2). There are gift shops, restaurants and bars in plenty, but you can easily escape into the extensive wooded picnic areas and quiet walkways nearby.

stays with the road for 0.4km before departing off left on a field track. On arriving at the main São Bartolomeu de Messines/Barranco do Velho road (38km), turn left.

Although this is a main road, the EN124 is in a poor state of repair in parts (especially further west around Benafim). First head for Salir and pass the point where Walk 15 again meets the main road from the left (38.5km) and continues on the track off right (38.9km). (The short version of Walk 15 crosses the road at the 39km-point.) The white water tower of Salir is easily distinguishable ahead, as you drive along past a scattering of white traditional houses. Take the left-hand turn up to **Salir** (♦✕📷☎; Picnic 15) at 42km; note that it is signposted to Loulé and comes up when you have almost passed the village. This road leads uphill and skirts round the village, which is on the left. Follow the road round, pass a left turn into the centre, and park on the roadside where it is fairly wide, about 0.9km from the main road. Head left up into the village to explore the centre — shown on page 32 — and perhaps enjoy the setting for Picnic 15. If you are doing Walk 15, park further along the wide road, about 1.3km from the main road (just before the T-junction and a right turn down to 'Ponte de Salir' and 'Loulé'). For more details about Salir, see the notes for Walk 15 on page 105.

Return to the main road by the same route to continue, and turn left. As you drive along (📷), you can't fail to notice the huge ridge of Rocha da Pena to the right (Walk 14). The village of Pena (☎), down the road off right after

48km, is the starting point for Walk 14 and Picnic 14. Since there isn't enough room to park in Pena, if you wish to stop now, or park to walk or picnic, leave your car tucked *well into the side* of this main road. **Benafim** is soon reached (51km), and here the road narrows to pass between the houses. After 55.8km, the narrow road off left is the return route on this tour — just before a sharp right-hand bend in the road, which can catch you unawares.

On entering the confines of Alte, at 56km, there is a road off right direct to Fonte Grande (Picnic 12). The main tour goes first into Alte and then on to Fonte Grande but, if you wish to go there straight away, turn right here, follow the road round and cross the bridge. This brings you to the first large fountain and small picnic area on the right. The much larger picnic area and fountain (Walk 12 and Picnic 12; photograph page 93), with better facilities, is to the right, past and above the first fountain.

We go first to explore the village itself, by continuing another 0.7km along the main road, past the Fonte Grande turn-off. The road runs below the village, which rises up to the right, and we cross a bridge where there is an old mill and some waterfalls. Turn right (as the main road bends round to the right), at the next road, which leads directly into the centre of Alte and the start of Walk 12. In

Cork oak

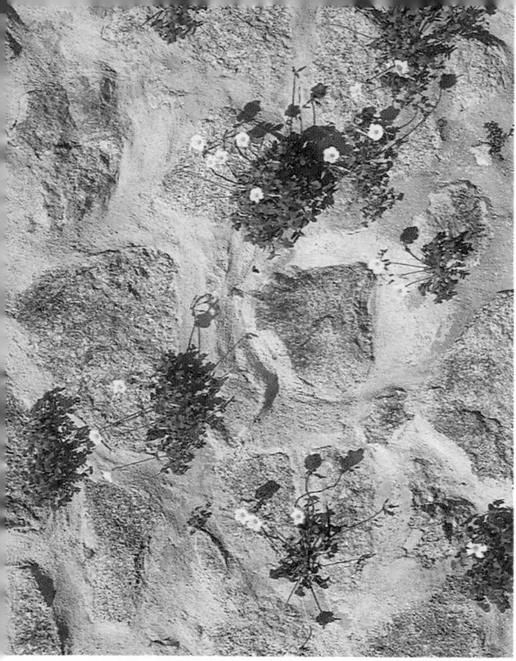

Bermuda buttercups at Monchique (Car tours 2 and 3; Walks 5 and 6)

just 0.2km, pass the left turn up to Santa Margarida (📷 and Walk 11, illustrated on pages 28-29, 88-89, 90-91) as you enter **Alte★** (✝⛪✕⛩📷☕). Park almost at once, where the road is wide (in the area of the fish market), and walk ahead into the centre. The slabs of the fish market stalls are on your left, and there are good views over the countryside to the right. From the centre continue to Fonte Grande through the very narrow village streets. Keep ahead to the centre, and go to the right and along the side of the church facing you. Turn right following the 'Fonte' signs; the road soon leads round left, to bring you out by the bridge and *fonte*. Keep ahead to drive to the main picnic area.

When you are ready to leave Alte, return to the main road (59km) and turn left. We've added 3km to the distance on arrival at this point, and we leave from the Santa Margarida end of Alte. Take care if you are leaving from the Santa Margarida end, as the road

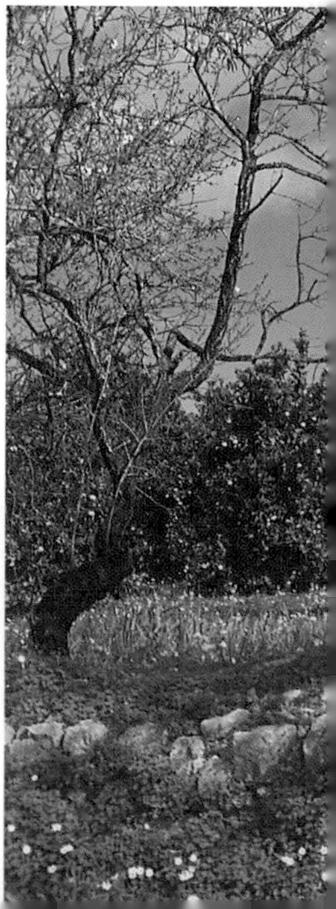

Orange groves on the drive up to Monte São Miguel (see page 46).

junction is on a bend which limits visibility, especially for a left turn. Retrace your route to the 55.8km point, just after a sharp left bend, and turn right into a narrow surfaced road (59.9km). The road now wends its way across the shallow valley south of Alte, through low-lying vegetation, which allows for good views () over the countryside. At the fork reached after 61.6km keep round to the right. Care is needed in the centre of the village of **Monte Brito**, where there is a right-angled bend and no view round the corner. As you drive along a straight stretch of road, it is easy to feel that you are on the major road but *beware*; in 65.2km a road joins from the right, and there is a 'STOP' sign for you to obey — with no road markings. This sign was *not* visible when we were there because of the surrounding foliage. Keep ahead, then turn right about 1km further on. You are now heading across country towards Paderne, where the church tower and buildings can be clearly seen in the distance. As you reach **Paderne** (69km ✝⊕🚐), keep to the road which skirts round to the right. On meeting the main road in Paderne, turn right downhill to meet the Bouliqueime road. Keep round to the right here, passing the cemetery on the left, which is a good place to stop and park to explore Paderne. A little further on there is the road down left to the 'Fonte' and Paderne Castle, which is the point where you park for Walk 13 and Picnic 13 (see photograph page 97).

To return to Faro, turn round and head in the direction of Bouliqueime, passing the road down from Paderne centre. (Those returning to Albufeira and environs should now continue to the main road at Purgatório, 0.5km further on, and turn left.) The road is narrow, but the countryside is very pretty along this route. Reach **Bouliqueime** and turn left onto the EN125 (79km) in the

This spectacular beach is on the route of Walk 10; it lies between the settings for Picnics 10a and 10b.

direction of Faro. The right turn to the airport is reached after 102km.

At the Faro ring road traffic lights (104km), turn left for 'Espanha' and 'Olhão' (or keep ahead for Faro centre). Turn right at the next traffic lights and, at the railway station, continue round to the left, to pass the bus station. Reach **Faro** centre after 106km.

> **BARREIRAS BRANCAS** 🚗 Circular walk for motorists ➤

This is a very short walk of 4km/2.5mi, taking about 45min, for those driving around the Loulé area. To get there, turn north at the central roundabout in Loulé (note the kilometre reading), to pass the bus station on the left. Then, at the crossroads before the monument, turn right, following the 'Querença' sign. This sets you on the Barranco do Velho road where, once beyond an avenue of cypress trees, look for a parking spot just before the start of a similar avenue (3km out of Loulé). Park on the right, near a small engineering works and opposite a café. A windmill on a hill is your destination.

Start the walk from the engineering works, by heading down the track between the workshop on the left and a house on the right. The track leads between orange groves to a bridge over a stream which is crossed in **2min**. Continue ahead, and ignore the track on the right as you start to ascend. Look for a walled-in trail, also on the right, reached in **7min**. Turn into this, and keep an eye out on the left for a narrower walled-in path within 2 minutes; it leads you up the hillside in a gentle ascent. This old route hides some interesting flowers like the broad-leaved *Epipactis helleborine* and the bright yellow *anemone palmata*. Stay ahead in **12min**, when the walled-in path runs into track and, as you continue to rise, you can enjoy views of Loulé to the right and the sea beyond. At the junction of tracks reached in **14min**, turn left in the direction of the windmill and, less than a minute later, stay ahead on a very rough track (where the main track swings right). Another fork in the track is quickly reached, where you keep left. Then, in **16min**, when the track divides (a right turn leads into a small quarry), stay ahead, to find that this track too ends almost immediately. From here a path leads through a stone wall on the right, up to the windmill, reached in **18min**. Whilst nothing much remains to see of the mill workings, there is a splendid panorama to be enjoyed from this location (see page 27). It is a good site for orchids, too, including the man orchid, *Aceras anthropophorum*, and the sombre bee orchid, *Ophrys fusca*.

Leave from the door of the mill and follow the path which heads in the direction of Loulé. Very shortly, when you reach a field, descend to meet the cross-path at the bottom (2min). Turn right to pass beneath the windmill, now up on the right. Keep ahead as the path runs into a rough track, and turn left at the track junction reached 2min later, to return briefly along the outward route. Stay ahead when a track joins from the right less than 2min later (used in the outward route) and continue to descend, taking care on this stony track. Turn right at the junction reached 11min below the mill and, with the way now easier underfoot, enjoy the rural surrounds. Cross a wide field track, to enter a walled-in trail ahead in 3min. Some 5min later, note the second of two walled-in paths leaving from the right: this is the path you took up to the mill. Turn left soon, to follow the outward route back to the car.

4 EASTERN HIGHLIGHTS

Faro • Olhão • (Tavira) • Vila Real de Santo António • Castro Marim • Cachopo • Barranco de Velho • São Bras de Alportel • Faro

182km/113.75mi; about 3 hours 30 minutes' driving: exit Faro from the harbour (see town plan pages 10-11).

On route: Picnics (see pages 12-16) 17, 20; Walks 16-20

Once off the mainly well-surfaced EN125, the inland roads become more winding and twisting, with some bumpy stretches. Make sure you have enough petrol before heading inland to Cachopo.

Vila Real is a bustling riverside town only a short ferry ride from Spain; nearby we find the tranquillity of a backwater, where the remains of a 14th-century castle stand sentinel to its past glory and importance. This tour penetrates deep into countryside still untouched by tourism, where you can relish an astoundingly beautiful landscape.

Start out from Faro as for Car tour 3 but, after turning left at the roundabout at the top of Avenida 5 de Outubro, turn right at the main traffic lights, signposted 'Espanha' (Spain). You are now on the EN125 which will take you all the way to Vila Real and the Spanish border.

Olhão (✝ ♠♠ ♠ ✕ △ ☕ ⊕ ☛ WC) is reached in 8km. Keep ahead on the main road at the first traffic lights but, if you want to explore Olhão, turn right here to reach the centre. (A left turn at the same point would take you out to Estói, setting for Walk 16.) Pass a left turn to Moncarapacho and São Bras and then a right turn to Porto de Olhão (9km). The port at Olhão is where you catch a ferry out to the barrier islands, where there are sandy beaches and shallow waters ideal for bathing— see top of page opposite. Beyond Olhão the road surface becomes very good until you reach **Luz de Tavira** (22km), where you need to take care, as the road narrows appreciably and the surface deteriorates. Once through Luz you're back on good road. Continue along through flat cultivated countryside and scattered hamlets, where oranges, almonds and vines are important crops. Just after

42

THE BARRIER ISLANDS

There is a group of islands and sand banks which lie offshore in the general area south and east of Faro and, if you fly into Faro airport, you will have an excellent overall view of them as you start to descend. The whole of this area is a nature reserve called 'Parque Natural da Ria Formosa'. The outermost islands are known as the 'barrier islands', since they protect the inland side from the worst of the rough seas, particularly when the Atlantic breakers are in full swell.

Two of the islands in the central area are popular for bathing. Both are reached by regular ferry from Olhão. The nearest, Ilha de Armona, is reached in about 15 minutes by ferry, and it is almost pure sand. The beach on the sheltered side runs into shallow, warm waters; it is an ideal family beach. The seaward side offers the longer beach — stretching almost all the way to Tavira. This means that you can almost always find a quiet spot of your own. The second island, Ilha da Culatra, is reached after a 45-minute ferry ride and has permanent habitation. Although just as beautiful, this island is generally less visited because of the longer ferry journey. Full details of the boat timetables are available from the tourist office in Olhão and from the ticket kiosk on the harbour.

Ilha de Armona is also accessible from Tavira. Frequent buses run from the square, Praça da Republica, and travel along the coast to connect up with the ferry, which runs constantly throughout the day in the season. This eastern end of the island has more facilities and is perhaps a little more crowded. Again, the inland side is well sheltered, and the seaward side enjoys the full force of the Atlantic. The most easterly of these barrier islands, Cabanas, can be reached from the town of Cabanas just to the east of Tavira.

petrol stations on both sides of the road (28km), the main road bends round to the left and Tavira ★ (♟ ⛪ ⛵ ✗ ⛱ ⌂ ☐ wc) is straight ahead. This is the first of a number of roads into Tavira. If you turn off before the high level bridge over the river, you will head into the main town. At the moment the old bridge (🏛) is closed to vehicular traffic, as a result of damage by flood water in the autumn of 1989. This means that you must return to the same point on the EN125 to continue. If you pass over the high level bridge before turning right into Tavira, you have to park and walk across the old bridge to the centre. Whichever way you choose, add about 3km to the overall distance for the tour, if you visit the town.

After the first turning to Tavira, reach a crossroads (29km) then a relatively new high-level road bridge. Note the left turn to Cachopo immediately after crossing the bridge; this is the road you will take on the return route. Pass crossroads (30km), where a right turn also leads to Tavira. Soon you are passing the large Eurotel complex on the left (32km), a landmark for those wishing to visit Tavira National Forest for Walk 19. The left turn to the forest is

0.3km after the Euro-tel and is signposted 'Mata Nacional' — but a 'Pension' sign indicating the same direction is more noticeable.

After some 40km, the road narrows and curves to cross a bridge, then speedily carries you on in the direction of Vila Real. Just after a water sports centre on the left (46km), there is a left turn to 'Castro Marim' and 'Beja' (our return route). Keep ahead on the main road, to come into **Vila Real de Santo António★** (‡🏔🏠✕🍴⊕M🚌WC), passing a second left turn to Castro Marim (52km). The road system in Vila Real is set out like a grid, so direction-finding is fairly straightforward. Follow the sign to the 'centro'; it directs you right, past the hospital on the left, and then left, down to the river. Entering on foot, you can follow the pedestrian walkway to the centre of town, by keeping ahead where the traffic is diverted to the right. Parking is allowed in some streets and along the riverside road. We found it easier to park on the outskirts and walk — especially if the town was busy. If you wish to visit Spain, a ferry crosses the river every 30 minutes, taking about 15 minutes to cross. The cost is very reasonable for both foot passengers and cars.

Return to the Castro Marim junction (at the 52km-point), and turn right. Gum and palm trees line the elevated road running straight through the nature reserve. Castro Marim itself can be clearly seen ahead. The start of Walk 20 is on the left, 1.6km from the junction with the EN125. Enter **Castro Marim★** (57km ‡📷🚌 WC; Picnic 20), and park on the right, past the church and just before the main road to Lisbon and Beja goes around to the right. Up to the right is the castle entrance. Picnic 20 is set inside the castle grounds, where there is also an information centre for the surrounding nature reserve. There are photographs of the area on pages 32-33, 127 and 128. Castro Marim is one of the best areas for bird-watching in Algarve; see notes on page 32 and also the notes for Walk 20.

Leave Castro Marim by following the signpost for Tavira — which means keeping ahead, instead of taking the main road to Lisbon which goes round to the right. At the point where a fork goes off right to 'Rio Seco' (59km), keep round to the left. Go over a level crossing (62km) and meet the EN125 after 64km, where you turn right in the direction of Faro. Keep on the EN125 as far as the high level bridge at Tavira (about 3km after the Eurotel complex on the right), and turn right towards Cachopo (81km). Keep right at the 'Picota' sign. The road is surfaced, but potholed and bumpy in parts. Initially, the road crosses a plain, with the river on the left, heading towards the hills.

Eucalyptus trees line the road as it starts to climb, passing the occasional vineyard and olive grove. Uniformly rounded hills roll into the distance as you penetrate this unknown but extremely photogenic area of Algarve (). A delightful and unusual mosaic, created by varying shades of vegetative cover, cloaks the landscape (◨), adding a delicious hint of unreality and adventure. Photographs of this area are on pages 25, 31 and 34-35. After 111km, you start to descend, to pass a café and cross the Ribeira de Odeleite. The changing scene is coloured by clusters of pink heather, *Erica australis*, as you pass a fountain on the right (115km). Just when you really begin to feel isolated and in the middle of nowhere, terraced hillsides, cleared of *matos*, announce the proximity of habitation. **Cachopo** (121km ♦ ✕ ⬛) is reached just after you pass an impressive cemetery on the right. Stretch your legs and explore this interesting backwater, untouched by tourism.

Leave Cachopo by turning left towards Barranco do Velho — in 1km looking out for a picturesque old stone bridge on the left. The road now wends along at a high level (◨) through the pleasant rural hamlets of **Catraia** and **Feiteira** to **Barranco**. Look for the windmill on the left (at 137km), before you start to descend into forest. When you reach **Barranco do Velho** (145km ⬛) a road goes off right towards Alte and São

Bartolomeu de Messines, but keep round left, to plunge down into the forest towards São Bras and Faro.

On reaching **São Bras** (158km ♁ 🏠 ♠ ✕ ⊕ ☎ WC; Walks 17 and 18; Picnic 17), keep ahead for Faro. If you wish to stop in São Bras, turn left into the square and park there, or take the next left turn out of the square, into the main shopping street to park. See the notes for Walk 17 (page 114) for more information about São Bras.

From São Bras, swiftly descend onto the plain, first passing the point where Walk 16 crosses the road on its return (162km), and then passing the left turn to Estoi. Walk 16 crosses here (165km), on its outward route. You regain Faro after 175km.

MONTE SÃO MIGUEL

Standing alone on the eastern side of Faro, this mound is a landmark which can be seen for miles around. It would be easy to identify even without the TV transmitter perched on the summit. It's not its height (only 410m/1350ft), but the fact that it stands on the edge of a large area of plain, that makes it so visible. Conversely, it is a good viewpoint, the best in the east. It doesn't offer anything in the way of walking possibilities, but it is worth the drive up to enjoy the views, if you are in the region. (The photograph on page 39 was taken during this drive.)

Perhaps you could combine this excursion with a visit to the Sunday market at Moncarapacho (see 'Country fairs and markets' on page 8). Moncarapacho lies 7km from the EN125 to the northwest of Olhão. Start out for São Miguel from Moncarapacho by heading north to Santa Catarina. After about 1km, fork left into a narrow surfaced road (where there is a hard-to-read signpost for São Miguel). This road leads all the way up to the summit, but be sure to keep left at the fork near the top. The distance to the summit from Moncarapacho is 5km. Apart from good views, there are some interesting wild flowers to be seen, if you make short forays into the *matos*.

☀ Walking

Algarve is justly famous for its fine beaches and beautiful coastline. It is not normally thought of in terms of open countryside, pretty villages and ideal rambling opportunities. Many visitors will be surprised by the fine and varied landscapes to be enjoyed across the length of the region. To the north and east, the rolling interlocking *matos*-covered hills catch the long rays of the sun, to present an ever-changing interplay of light and shade. The limestone of the central Barrocal plays host to most of the charming villages — and to the best of the wild flowers. Further west, the granite mountains of the Serra de Monchique provide the ruggedness and grandeur. Further west still, the landscape takes on a windswept appearance, which is at its most extreme as you approach Sagres. It is impossible to ignore the fine coastline, and we have made the most of those parts which are still unspoilt, so that you can enjoy some of the scenery which has contributed to the fame of this beautiful region.

There is walking enough to keep you occupied throughout the whole of a two-week holiday — and to tempt you back for more. All the groundwork has been done, so straight from day one you can be out in the countryside, enjoying your holiday to the full. But please accept some words of caution. Follow the walks as described, and never try to get from one walk to another across uncharted terrain — even though it may look possible. Distances in mountains are very deceptive, and points that look close can sometimes take many hours of walking to bridge.

There are walks in this book for everyone. All walks are graded, so just check the grade to see if it suits you and, if the grade of the main walk is too advanced, be sure to check all the shorter versions.

If you are an inexperienced walker, or if you are just looking for a gentle walk, then go for the walks graded 'easy'. Try perhaps the coastal walks, where you can go only as far as you like, before returning. Look too at the picnic suggestions on pages 13-16, which visit a selection of particularly beautiful spots — many of which are easily reached in under an hour's walking.

Experienced walkers should be able to tackle all of the

47

walks in this book, taking into account, of course, the season and the weather conditions. If a walk is very long, do be sure of your fitness before you attempt it. Don't attempt the more strenuous walks in high summer; do protect yourself from the sun, and always carry an ample supply of water and plenty of fruit with you. Always remember that storm damage could make some of the walks described in this book unsafe, so be sure to err on the side of safety. If you have not reached one of our landmarks after a reasonable time, then you must return to the last 'sure' point and start again.

For **expert walkers**, the walks around Monchique offer the best challenge and, if you are out to test your stamina, it is possible to join some walks together to make a longer day.

G uides, waymarking, maps

Official **guides** are not available, but none is needed for the walks in this book. Most of the walks use well established footpaths, trails and tracks, and are easily followed.

There is no official **waymarking**. Waymarks are sometimes seen along some of the walks but, generally, these are not helpful. In some areas coloured arrows painted on walls are used to show the way to houses which are off the beaten track. To avoid any possible confusion, it is wiser to follow our directions at all times, in preference to any route markings.

The **maps** in this book are the most useful you will find for guiding you through the walks. They are reproductions of old 1:50,000 maps, which we have updated by adding roads and some *major* tracks. Obviously, at this scale, it is not possible to include all footpaths and minor tracks. These old maps, produced in the 1950s and 60s by the Instituto Geográfico e Cadastral, are still available. If you want to see larger areas of mapping, they can be purchased from Stanfords in London (12 Long Acre, London WC2E 9LP). The region is covered by fourteen sheets.

W hat to take

If you are already in Portugal when you find this book, and you haven't any special equipment such as a rucksack and walking boots, you can still do some of the walks — but better still, buy some of the equipment you need locally. Boots, shoes, and trainers can all be bought fairly cheaply, provided you do not require a large size. Continental size 45 is often the upper limit for men and 41 for women. Don't attempt any of the difficult walks without the proper gear or with brand new footwear. For each walk in the book, the *minimum* year-round equipment is listed. Where walking boots are required there is, unfortunately, no substitute: you will need to rely on the grip and ankle support they provide, and they are absolutely essential on some walks where the path descends steeply over loose stones. All other walks should be made with stout shoes, preferably with thick rubber soles to grip on wet and slippery surfaces. Occasionally, where we feel the walk is suitable for trainers, then they have been included as an option. You may find the following check list useful:

walking boots (which must be
   broken-in and comfortable)
waterproof rain gear
   (outside summer months)
long-sleeved shirt
   (for sun protection)
long trousers, tight at the ankles
   (sun and tick protection)
plastic groundsheet
antiseptic cream
woollen hat and gloves
water bottle with water
   purifying tablets
'dog dazer' (see 'Things that
   bite or sting', page 51)

spare boot laces
bandages and band aids
plastic plates, cups, etc
knives and openers
anorak (zip opening)
sunhat, sunglasses
universal sink plug
protective suncream
insect repellent
two cardigans
extra pair (long) socks
compass, whistle, torch
small rucksack
binoculars
compact folding umbrella

Please bear in mind that we have not done *every* walk in the book under *all* conditions. We might not realise just how hot or exposed some walks might be in high summer or how cold in winter. For this reason we have listed under 'Equipment' all the gear you *might* need, depending on the season, and we rely on your good judgement to modify the list accordingly.

Beware of the sun and the effects of dehydration. Don't be deceived by light cloud cover; you can still get sunburnt. It's tempting to wear shorts for walking, forgetting that, with the sun behind you, the backs of your legs and your neck are getting badly sunburnt. Pushing through prickly holly oak in shorts isn't much fun either. Always carry long trousers and a long-sleeved shirt and put them on when you have had enough sun — and *always* wear a sunhat. Choose a shady spot for your lunch on hot days, and make sure that you carry with you a good supply of fruit and water.

Where to stay

There is a wide range of resorts to suit all tastes in Algarve, with virtually all of them situated along the coast. The **central part of the coastline** is a good area in which to stay, because you can get around to most parts of Algarve without too much travelling. **Albufeira** is the largest resort in this region, and it has very good bus connections, although it is not so convenient for trains. The nearest station is at Ferreira, which is about 6km/3.75mi outside the resort. For a quieter resort, try some of the smaller places outside Albufeira.

Moving **westwards**, **Carvoeiro** is another lively resort, which is a convenient base for exploring the western part of the region, and where we stayed while based in the west. If you prefer smaller, quieter places, then look **west of Portimão**. For years the bridge at Portimão has been a bottleneck for traffic and has been very effective in limiting holiday developments to the west. A new bridge is currently under construction, which is causing even more havoc with the traffic at the moment but, when it is eventually finished, it will ease the traffic problem which is at its worst in high season. **Lagos** is a pleasing resort, which seems to combine spaciousness with the peace of somewhere much smaller. Once west of Lagos, the resorts get progressively quieter and more unspoilt.

For exploring the **eastern side of the region**, we made our base at **Faro**. While it does not have the traditional image of a resort, it is an interesting place to stay and a convenient centre for public transport. **Olhão**, to the east of Faro, is even less easy on the eye, but convenient for boats out to the beautiful beaches of the barrier islands. **Tavira**, possibly the most picturesque resort on the eastern side, is also a centre for boat trips out to the barrier islands. **Monte Gordo**, almost on the eastern border with Spain, is also a popular resort, but from here few of the walks are within easy reach.

The old irrigation wells bring a charm to the countryside.

Weather

The kindest months for walking in this part of Portugal are those either side of summer: March, April, May, September and October. However, walking through the mild winter months can be entirely delightful. There can be many fine days, even in January, which are quite superb for walking. February, too, can provide many good opportunities and, in 1990, it proved to be the equal of any of the later spring months. By March the temperature is starting to rise, and it is certainly warm enough to air the shorts. Sunny days are plentiful, but there is still a chance of a day or two with rain, and these conditions prevail through April, even though the temperature is increasing steadily. May brings more warmth and sunshine, with only a small risk of unsettled weather. By June the weather is getting too hot for strenuous walks, but some of the coastal walks, where you will be cooled by the Atlantic sea breezes, can still be enjoyed — as they can throughout the summer months.

As the summer heat starts to decline in September, a new walking season opens up. This lasts through October and into November — until the start of the rainy season. The late autumn is often the wettest part of the year, and this was especially true in 1989. Much of the damage caused then by the heavy rains is still to be seen along the route of some of the walks described in this book. (However, 1989 was an exceptional year, since the average rainfall for the area, especially the coastal region, is very low, at 400-500mm per annum.)

Things that bite or sting

Dogs can be a nuisance. We were thankful to be carrying a 'dog dazer', which we found to be very effective, and it gave us considerable confidence. A dog dazer is a small, easily portable electronic device which, on the press of a button, emits a noise which is inaudible to the human ear, but which startles aggressive dogs and persuades them to back off. For information about the dog dazer, write to Dazer UK, Freepost, London SW11 6BR. Otherwise, the best advice, if you feel threatened and have no walking stick, is to pick up a stone and pretend to throw it. More often than not, the dogs bark loudly but are rarely actually aggressive.

Snakes are something you will have to be on your guard against. We saw very few throughout the spring months, but we are advised that there are more around in summer. Most are probably harmless, but if there are any of the viper species around, then great care is needed. Most snakes are more frightened of you than you are of them, and they will move out of your way rapidly. But, if they don't, the best advice is to move quietly out of their way. The real danger comes should you accidentally step on a snake. For this reason, it is *imperative* that you do not walk in the countryside in open sandals, no matter how comfortable they might be for walking. Always have your feet and ankles well covered. It is also a sensible precaution to wear your long trousers tucked into your socks. Take special care near water, when you are about to sit down, or when you choose to rest your hand, so unthinkingly, on a dry-stone wall.

Scorpions are around, too, but you are most likely to see them in the height of summer, when they are usually seeking shade — so don't leave any of your clothing on the ground. Accidentally turning over rocks or stones may expose them but, generally, they offer no serious threat, since their sting is more painful than dangerous for most people.

In areas which are well forested, **ticks** can be a problem. As you brush through the woodlands, they can get onto your clothes. Again, if you follow our advice about wearing long trousers and a long-sleeved shirt, you should be able to keep them off your skin. If they do manage to get to your skin, then it is necessary to make them withdraw before you take them off. An easy way to do this is to touch them with a solvent such as methylated spirits or petrol.

Bees and **wasps** are around in summer, so make sure you carry the necessary creams and pills, especially if you are allergic to insect bites.

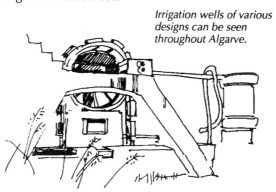

Irrigation wells of various designs can be seen throughout Algarve.

Portuguese for walkers

Despite the large numbers of tourists that visit Algarve, British tourists in particular, we found surprisingly little English spoken outside the major resorts. To ask directions in the countryside, you may well need to try your hand at Portuguese. A good technique is to memorise a few key questions, and then try to phrase your question so that it demands a 'yes' (*sim*) or 'no' (*não*) answer. It is not always possible to conduct the whole conversation in this manner, so it pays to learn a few other answers that you might expect, or which you can use to form more questions to get yes/no answers. Examples of key questions and possible answers are given below.

Key questions

English	Portuguese	approximate pronunciation
Pardon me,	Faz o favor,	Fahz oh fah-**vohr**,
sir (madam).	senor (senhora).	sehn-**yohr** (sehn-**yoh**-rah).
Where is	Onde é	**Ohn**-deh eh
the footpath to ...	a verada para ...	ah veh-**ray**-dah **pah**-rah ...
(the main road to ...	(a estrada para...	(ah ish-**trah**-dah **pah**-rah ...
the way to...	o caminho para...	oh cah-**mee**-noh **pah**-rah ...
the bus stop)?	a paragem)?	ah pah-**rah**-jeng?
Many thanks.'	Muito obrigado.	**Mween**-toh oh-bree-**gah**-doh
	(a woman says	
	muito obriga<u>da</u>).	(oh-bree-**gah**-<u>dah</u>).

Possible answers

English	Portuguese	approximate pronunciation
here	aqui	ah-**key**
there	ali	ah-**lee**
straight ahead	sempre em frente	**sem**-preh em **frenght**
behind	atras	ah-**trahsh**
to the right	a dereita	ah deh-**ray**-tah
to the left	a esquerda	ah ish-**kehr**-dah
above	em cima	engh **see**-mah
below	em baixo	engh **bigh**-joh

Try to get a native speaker (possibly somebody at the hotel or a taxi driver) to help you learn the pronunciation. You must pronounce *very carefully* the name of your destination. For guidance with the pronunciation of place names in this book, see the Index, beginning on page 134.)

When you have your mini-speech memorised, always ask the many questions that you can concoct from it in such a way that a yes/no answer will result. *Never* ask an open-ended question such as 'Where is the main road?' and leave it at that! Unless you are actually standing on it, you will not understand the answer! Instead, ask the question then suggest the most likely answer yourself, for example:

'Faz o favor, senhora. Onde é a estrada para Faro? É sempre em frente?' or 'Faz o favor, senhor. Onde é a verada para Alte? É em cima a esquerda?'

If you go through your list of answers, you will eventually get a yes — with a vigorous nod of the head — and it will be a lot more reliable than just sign language.

An inexpensive phrase book, such as those published by Collins, Berlitz or Hugo, is a very valuable aid from which you can choose other 'key' phrases and answers. Remember, too, that it is always nice to greet people you may meet on your walks with a 'good morning' or 'good afternoon' (bom dia/bohm **dee**-ah) or (boa tarde/boah **tar**-day).

Walkers' checklist

The following points cannot be stressed too often:
- **At any time a walk may become unsafe** due to storms or bulldozing. If the route is not as we describe it, and your way ahead is not secure, *do not attempt to go on.*
- **Never walk alone** — four is the best walking group.
- **Do not overestimate your energies** — your pace will be determined by the slowest walker in the group.
- **Transport** connections at the end of the walk are very important.
- Proper **footwear** and **sun protection** is mandatory.
- **Mists** can suddenly appear in the mountains.
- **Warm clothing** is needed in the mountains; even in summer, take some along, in case you are delayed.
- **Compass, whistle, torch** weigh little, but might save your life.
- **Extra ration**s must be taken on long walks.
- A **stout stick** is a help on rough terrain and to discourage the rare unchained, menacing dog.
- **Review** the 'Important note' on page 2, as well as grade and equipment for each walk, before you set out.

Organisation of the walks

The twenty major walks in this book are spread across the whole of Algarve, with the greatest concentration towards the central area. You might begin by considering the large fold-out touring map between pages 16 and 17. Here you can see at a glance the overall terrain, the road network, and the exact orientation of the walking maps in the text. Quickly flipping through the pages, you will find that there is at least one photograph for each walk.

Having selected one or two potential excursions from the map and the photographs, look over the planning information at the beginning of each walk. Here you'll find *our* walking times, grade, equipment, and how to get there and return. If the grade and equipment specifications are beyond your scope, don't despair! There's almost always a short or alternative version of the walk and, in most cases, these are less demanding of ability and equipment. If it still looks too strenuous for you, turn to pages 13-16, where the picnic suggestions allow you to savour a walk's special landscape with the minimum of effort.

When you are on the walk, you'll find that the text begins with an introduction to give you a flavour of the landscape and comments about special points of interest, before the route is described in detail. The text is illustrated with large scale maps (all 1:50,000 and all with north at the top). These have been adapted to show current routes and key landmarks.

Note that **we are very fit walkers** and that our times average between 3 and 6 kilometres an hour. Also note that the times given are *walking* times and include only brief pauses, where you might stop to recover breath. They do not include photographic or picnic stops — or any stops of indeterminate length. So, if you are a beginner or simply out for a more leisurely stroll, **a walk may take you up to twice as long as the stated time**. Don't forget to take bus connections at the end of the walk into account, particularly with regard to the last bus of the day. The most important factor is *consistency* of walking times, and we have made an effort to check our times at least twice. You'll soon see how your pace compares with ours and make adjustments for your stride ... and the heat!

Many of the **symbols** used on the walking maps are self-explanatory, but here is a key to the more important ones:

⎯⎯ RED ⎯⎯ main (red) road on the touring map	⛪ church	● *fonte*, tank, well, etc ▼
⎯⎯ RED ⎯⎯ secondary (white) road on touring map	◼ castle, fort	�𝕀𝕀 site, ruins
═══ tracks (not all are on the touring map)	✚ shrine	→ direction of the walk
═══	✳ windmill	
GREEN route of the walk	🚗 car parking	⤢ quarry
GREEN alternative walk	🚌 bus stop	0 ⊢⎯⎯⎯⎯⊣ 1 km
	∪ lime oven	⊢⎯⎯⎯⊣ ½ mi

1 LUZ • ATALAIA • PORTO DE MÓS • PONTA DA PIEDADE • LAGOS

Distance: 9.3km/5.8mi; 2h

Grade: easy-moderate. The walk is mainly on footpaths, some climbing involved especially in the first part from Luz to the obelisk at 108m/355ft.

Equipment: sturdy shoes or boots, long-sleeved shirt, shorts or long trousers, swimming costume, binoculars, sunglasses, suncream, cardigan, raingear, picnic, water

How to get there: 🚌 by bus from Lagos to Luz (Timetable 1). Journey time 11min. 🚗 by car: Immediately on entering Luz follow the sign off left to 'Praia da Luz', down to a car park by the sea front. If you do arrive by car, the chances are that you will have to walk back the same way: see 4 below.

Short walks: These shorter walks fall into the easy grade, but they both require the same equipment.

1 To the obelisk (*atalaia*) above Luz and return (2.8km/1.75mi; 36min; a stiff climb). Follow the start of the walk and return the same way.

2 To Porto de Mós and return (8.8km/5.5mi; 1h50min). Follow the main walk for 53min, and make this your turning point. There is a café/bar where you can take refreshments before returning. The beach is stony close to the path, but sandy further out.

Alternative walks

3 To Ponta da Piedade and return (12.8km/8mi; 2h45min). Follow the main walk to the lighthouse; return the same way. Easy-moderate.

4 Luz — Lagos — Luz (18.6km/11.5mi; 4h). If you go by car, you may have to walk back the same way, because of the limited bus services between Lagos and Luz (Timetable 1). Easy-moderate.

5 Porto de Mós — Ponta da Piedade — Porto de Mós (4.0km/2.5mi; 1h). This option is available only if you are travelling by car or taxi. Park in the large car park at Porto de Mós and from here walk to the lighthouse at Ponta da Piedade. Use the notes for the main walk (from the 53min-point), and return the same way. To get to Porto de Mós: on approaching Lagos from Portimão, immediately you cross the bridge, continue ahead at the roundabout, following signs for Sagres. Keep ahead to the T-junction, where Luz/Sagres are signposted right. Turn *left* here, and then right 1.4km later, following the sign to Porto de Mós (2km).

Longer walks: The coastal footpath stretches all the way from Lagos to Salema. We have broken the route down into three stretches which are presented as Walks 1-3. All the sections have a totally different character with different points of interest and, if you want to spend a little time on the various beaches, exploring the villages or relaxing in the café/bars, then they are worth doing separately. But they can be joined together in various combinations — as in the following. See map pages 62-63.

6 Salema to Luz via Burgau (10.1km/6.3mi; 2h40min). Taxi or bus to Salema (Timetable 2) and walk back to Luz using the notes from Walks 3 and 2 consecutively. Return from Luz by bus (Timetable 1).

7 Burgau to Lagos via Luz (14km/8.7mi;3h10min). Take a bus out to Burgau, as detailed in Walk 2, and walk back to Lagos, using the notes for Walks 2 (in reverse) and 1 consecutively.

8 Salema to Lagos (19.5km/12.1mi; 4h40min). Take a taxi or bus out to Salema (Timetable 2) and walk the whole distance back to Lagos using the notes for Walks 3, 2 (in reverse) and Walk1 consecutively.

oastal footpaths always have great appeal, and this one is no exception. The moods of the sea, the play of light, a weaving coastline, the tang of salt, secluded bays all help to etch them firmly into the memory. Fine views from the obelisk (*atalaia*) above Luz are one of the highlights of this walk, as is the lighthouse and the egretry at Ponta da Piedade. The interest at this point is the spectacular rugged coastline and the stacks around the coast (see photograph on the next page).

Luz itself is a delightful and relatively small fishing village lying to the west of Lagos. It is slowly developing as a tourist resort. For the moment it is still quite small, but boasts good facilities in terms of restaurants and cafés. There are some fine beaches from where you can swim or enjoy water sports such as windsurfing.

Interesting wild flowers, including orchids, can be found all along this part of the coast, and a description of these is included in Walk 2.

Start the walk from the car park by the sea at the eastern side of the village by turning left towards the obelisk that you can see on the headland. Follow the cobbled road to the T-junction reached in under **1min,** where you turn right. At the second T-junction, a minute later, turn left, away from the shore. As the cobbled road ends, stay ahead on the rough track and follow it up the hillside. Soon, after **5min**, the track is leading you towards the obelisk, and you can see a path heading directly up the steepest part of the hillside. It is better *not* to take this path, but to use the diagonal approach which is more gradual. Take the left fork, reached in **8min**, and head towards the ruined building visible on top of the hill. Erosion has made the footpaths difficult in parts, so some care is needed. The slow ascent at least gives you time to scan the hillside for flowers. After **15min**, just before you reach the ruined building, go up right to join a field track and turn right to the obelisk (**20min**).

From the *atalaia* there are some fine views to enjoy over Luz and along the coast, as well as along the valley inland. Continue from here by following the track past the obelisk, heading in the direction of Lagos. The track reduces to more of a wide path as you dip through a hollow (**21min**), and back to the cliff-tops. The walking soon becomes fairly level for a time, at a height of about 75m/250ft, and you gain views of Lagos ahead — as well as the lighthouse. In **48min**, just at the start of the descent to Porto de Mós, a track joins from the left. Continue

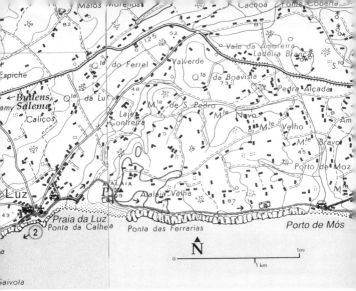

ahead, taking care on this badly eroded track. You reach Porto de Mós in **53min**.

Head for the restaurant on the far side of the bay and pass it on the beach side. Climb the steps to the left, immediately behind the restaurant, and turn right to join the next section of coastal path. The path leads uphill straight away and, in **56min**, as you approach some tall American agaves, it is easier to divert left as the path divides to reach the top. From here a narrow path leads along the cliff-top, with villas over to the left. A wide gully is reached in **1h**. Paths do lead across it, but erosion and damage to the steps on the far side make climbing up the other side a bit of a scramble, so the easier way is to stay on the path which skirts the gully to the left. This

From the lighthouse at Ponta da Piedade it is well worth a walk out over the bridge to the rocky headland, but those who suffer from vertigo should not go beyond the bridge. Nearer the lighthouse, good views can be had if you have the energy to descend the steps to the landing stage, where boat trips from Praia Dona Ana land their passengers. Look carefully at the various stacks to identify the one used by the egrets as their breeding ground. It came as a surprise and delight to us to find that there are still regions of Algarve which remain unspoilt and where fine coastal walks are possible. Another such walk, further east, is described in Walk 10.

emerges on a road three minutes later, where you turn right and, a minute later, right again back onto the cliff-top, to rejoin the coastal path in **1h05min**. Two minutes later pass a campsite on the left. Now the path undulates slightly, before we reach the lighthouse at Ponta da Piedade (**1h22min**).

The final stage into Lagos is mainly road walking. Continue around the lighthouse to the car park (**1h24min**; restaurant/bar in season). Follow the Lagos road past the car park; then take the path on the right (**1h26min**). It wanders a little away from the road, to cross another surfaced road (**1h34min**) near a restaurant on the right at Camilo. From here it heads diagonally back to the Lagos road across a rocky, sandy area, rejoining it through gate posts (**1h38min**). Turn right here. Keep ahead at the junction (**1h40min**; but divert right if you want to see the small resort and lovely beach at Praia Dona Ana) and swing right through the city walls ten minutes later. Follow the one-way system through the old town, turning left at the traffic lights (**1h55min**). The main square comes into view five minutes later.

2 LUZ • BURGAU • LUZ

Distance : 9.5km/5.9mi; 2h10min

Grade: easy. There is only one significant climb over a headland, and the footpaths, although stony in parts, are mostly good.

Equipment: sturdy shoes or boots, long-sleeved shirt, shorts or long trousers, swimming costume, sunglasses, suncream, cardigan, raingear, picnic, water

How to get there: 🚌 by bus from Lagos to Luz (Timetable 1). Journey time 11min. 🚗 by car: Immediately on entering Luz, follow the sign off left to Praia da Luz, to descend to a car park by the sea front.
To return: 🚌 from Luz to Lagos (Timetable 1), or car

Short walk: Luz to Burgau (4.7km/2.9mi; 1h5min; same grade, requires the same equipment as the main walk). Follow the notes for the main walk to Burgau. Return from Burgau to Lagos by bus departing Burgau weekdays at 11.27, 17.45; Sundays at 14.30.

Longer walk: See Walk 1 for details of longer walks, including the option of walking between Luz and Salema.

T his section of coastal path, westwards from Luz, is the easiest and the shortest. Although there are no sandy bays en route, Burgau awaits you, with its long stretch of beach — fine for swimming or just relaxing. See Walks 1 and 3 for more about the villages of Luz and Burgau.

Start the walk from the car park at the sea front on the eastern side of the village. Set out westward, away from the obelisk, along the promenade. Turn right at the end of

About 40 minutes into the walk: an Agave americana is shown in the foreground of the photograph. This plant was introduced into the Mediterranean area from Mexico over two centuries ago. Now it is widely naturalised, — even on the southwestern Atlantic coast.

There is a wealth of wild flowers to be found along the whole of this coastal path from Lagos to Salema. Without doubt the best display is in the spring, but many plants, especially the cistus and other shrubs, do have a more prolonged flowering period. Limestone bluffs, eroded valleys offering protection for the plants from the wind and the salt, and deep-red coarse sandy soils are some of the different habitats which are to be seen. Orchids are particularly common in the limestone regions, and the short grass hides many bee orchids, including the bumblebee orchid, *Ophrys bombyliflora*, the yellow bee orchid, *O lutea*, and the mirror orchid, *O speculum* — as well as the tongue orchid, *Serapias parviflora*. Less common are two charming narcissus — *N bulbocodium*, which resembles a small daffodil, and the tiny jonquil, *N gaditanus*. Still on limestone, one interesting plant to see all year round is the dwarf fan palm, *Chamaerops humilis*. This is the only native European palm; it rarely develops a stem, and the flowers are hidden in a dense cluster of leaves.

Common all along the cliffs, where it often forms neat mounds, is the yellow-flowered *Asteriscus maritimus*, which belongs to the daisy family. Cistus, too, are well represented, with the pink-flowered *Cistus albidus*, the white-flowered sage-leaved cistus, *Cistus salvifolius*, and *Halimium commutatum*, a rock rose with clear yellow flowers. An annual of the same family is the spotted rock rose, *Tuberaria guttata*, which has small yellow flowers with a dark brown centre. The iris are so widespread that they are certain to be noticed — but possibly only after lunch, since *Iris sisyrinchium* opens its flowers only around mid-day. Two more to mention in this short list, both fairly common, are sweet alison, *Lobularia maritima*, with its fragrant small white flowers, and the blue-flowered tassel hyacinth, *Muscari comosum*.

the promenade to pass a church on your right (**5min**) and then, almost immediately, take the first road left. This sets you heading towards the open country. The road runs into track in **9min** and, when the track ends six minutes later, take the path which leads diagonally left towards the seashore.

Like giant red paving slabs, the rock strata on the left slopes away into the sea, while the footpath stays safely inland. Be sure to watch out and avoid the three deep holes on the left (passed in **19min**). From here the path leads you left around a raised flat area, to end up at a slightly higher level (**23min**). As you reach the rocky bay (**26min**), follow the path uphill to the right, towards a villa and, two minutes later, just as you reach the house, follow the path away to the left to join a field track. The track, which follows the coastline, slowly narrows, so that in **38min** you are on a path heading up the centre of the hill ahead. Looking back you can see the obelisk at Luz and, beyond it, the lighthouse near Lagos. Close at hand you should find fan-leaved palms and the much taller American agaves shown opposite.

There is a short steep climb to contend with, but new vistas open up as you reach the top (**41min**). Burgau lies on the far side of the windmill which you can see ahead and, on a clear day, it is possible to see all along the coastline to Sagres. Take care on the stony footpath, as you descend to continue along the cliff-edge. The cliffs fall steeply into the sea here, and shortly you find that you are walking along a wide rocky ledge which narrows in parts. Vertigo sufferers can avoid this section by following the edge of the field on the right. The area where you pass the windmill (**53min**) makes a good picnic spot, but lacks shade.

Some five minutes later, as you approach the pens on the outskirts of Burgau, head up to the right to join a rough track and follow it, to pass the pens on your left. Burgau comes into view **1h** into the walk. The track runs into road, as you swing right to descend into the village. (Note two tracks here; take the lower one on your return). As you enter the village (**1h03min**), turn left towards the sea, passing toilets on your right, and continue right along the shore into the fishing harbour, shown on page 30 (**1h05min**).

Return the same way or, if you are doing the shorter version, head up the narrow street from the harbour to find the bus stop.

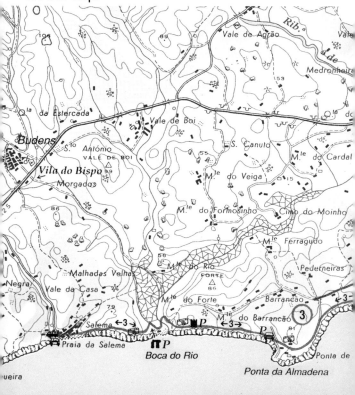

3 BURGAU • PONTA DA ALMADENA • BOCA DO RIO • SALEMA • BURGAU

Distance : 11km/6.8mi; 3h

Grade: moderate. This coastal walk is full of headlands to negotiate so there are quite a few ups and downs. Some of the footpaths are stony and can be difficult.

Equipment: sturdy shoes or boots, long-sleeved shirt, shorts or long trousers, swimming costume, sunglasses, suncream, cardigan, raingear, picnic, water

How to get there: 🚌 by bus from Lagos to Burgau (Timetable 1). Journey time 19min. 🚗 by car: As you reach Burgau, turn right into the wide road to park. Don't attempt to take the car down the narrow streets to the sea front.

To return: 🚌 bus from Burgau to Lagos, departs Burgau weekdays 11.27, 17.45; Sundays 10.05, 14.30, or car

Short walks: All require the same equipment as above.

1 Burgau — Ponta da Almadena — Burgau (4.6km/2.9mi; 1h10min). This one is easy, but there is still some climbing and problems with stony paths. Follow the notes for the main walk for the first 35min, until you reach the small sheltered beach at Ponta da Almadena. There is a café there for food and drinks. Return the same way.

2 Burgau — Boca do Rio — Burgau (7.6km/4.75mi; 2h). Moderate. Use the notes for the main walk to go to the beach at Boca do Rio, where there are some Roman remains. Return the same way.

3 Burgau to Salema (5.5km/3.4mi; 1h27min). Moderate. Follow the notes for the main walk all the way to Salema, and return from there by bus to Lagos (see Timetable 2).

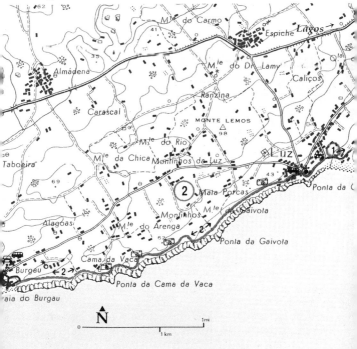

Burgau (see photograph page 30) is one of the few fishing villages in Algarve which still retains its charm and character. The main street of the village runs down to the sea, where fishing boats provide plenty of colour. This walk along the cliffs to Salema is very much like travelling a switch-back — you climb the bluffs only to descend the other side. The two small beaches encountered en route make good resting places, although the beach at Ponta da Almadena all but disappears at high tide.

The bus stops at the corner of the wide road (where there is also room to park). **Start the walk** from the bus stop by heading down the wide street with the sea over on your left. After **3min**, as you leave the houses behind, take the path on the left which leads to the headland. It is a steepish climb to start, but the spring flowers give good reason to pause (see comments in Walk 2). Once up on the headland, after **6min**, you enjoy fine views back towards Lagos. The obelisk above Luz and the lighthouse near Lagos can both be seen. Follow the path by the cliff-top as it dips down through a hollow. Over to the right farmhouses dot the barren countryside. There is another dip to cross and, as you rise again, the path runs into a rough track (**12min**). Keep ahead on the track by the coast, to get good views of the shingle beaches below. In **25min** you can see Salema ahead and the Sagres headland in the distance. In **29min** the track descends through a cutting, to meet a cross-track a minute later. Turn sharp right here, but turn off this track in under a minute, to descend a path to a small cove at Ponta da Almadena (**35min**). The café/bar at the back of the sandy beach has such a beautiful outlook that it is hard to pass by, thirsty or not!

Cross the beach to continue, but head towards the sea, to pick up the path that continues along the coast. There is an initial short steep climb but, by **39min**, you are back on the top again. Ahead you can see an old fort but, before you get there, there is a house to negotiate. As you meet the wall (**40min**), turn down right to keep alongside it and skirt the house (now on your left). Pick up the coastal path again beyond here and head towards the fort on the cliff-edge. Keep right when there is a choice of paths just before the fort, to reach it in **50min**. Pass through the enclosure and out the other side to continue. Stay with the coastal path as it swings to the right and starts into a steep descent towards the bay of Boca do Rio, lying at the mouth of a flat-bottomed valley. In **56min**, just before the bottom of the valley, the path joins a very rough track by a ruin on the left

Picnic 3b: looking back towards the fort across the beach at Boca do Rio. Just out of sight, in the foreground, lie some Roman ruins.

(note this carefully for the return). Turn left and follow this track down to the riverside, where you swing right towards the concrete foot-bridge (**59min**) and cross the river. Inland from here is a good area for bird-watching.

After crossing the bridge, the path heads towards the shore but meets a field track almost immediately, where you turn right inland (but turn left to go down to the shore or to inspect the fenced-off area which protects the remains of a Roman settlement). Shortly (**1h01min**), where the field track joins a stabilised track, turn right to continue around the perimeter of the fence. At the junction reached two minutes later, turn left back towards the sea, still skirting the fence. The track heads away from the fence, to take you back onto the coastal route again. In **1h11min**, as the main track swings inland, take the smaller track on the left, which continues to follow the coastline (photograph above). Salema looks tantalisingly close. Inland there are good views towards Monchique, where the twin peaks of Foia (Walks 4 and 5) and Picota (Walk 8) can be seen. After passing behind a house (**1h20min**)*, leave the track to take a path on the left, which soon swings right down between the houses. It emerges three minutes later on Rua dos Pescadoros (by No 13). Turn left to go down to the sea-front, with its beach, restaurants and cafés (**1h27min**).

Return the same way.

*The house reached in 1h20min was still under construction at the time of writing, and the footpath off left here might be disrupted. Another, less distinct path starts just before the house is reached. Since it is closer to the cliff-edge, be especially careful, before joining onto our route.

4 FONTE (FOIA) • MADRINHA • PÉ DO FRIO • CHILRÃO • FONTE (FOIA)

Distance: 12.5km/7.8mi; 3h   **See map pages 72-73**

Grade: moderate-strenuous. There is a descent of 375m/1230ft in the first part which has to be regained on the return. The footpaths and tracks used are generally good underfoot.

Equipment: sturdy shoes or boots, long-sleeved shirt, long trousers, sunglasses, suncream, cardigan, raingear, picnic, water

How to get there and return: 🚗 only accessible by car. From Monchique follow the signs for Foia and park at the *miradouro* on the left reached 6km after leaving the Monchique road. There is more parking space also on the left just 200m further on.

Shorter walks: Both require the same equipment as above.

1 Fonte — Madrinha — Fonte (3.6km/2.25mi; 1h10min). Easy grade, but not easy walking. Follow the notes for the main walk to enjoy the views from the summit of Madrinha and return the same way.

2 Fonte — Pé do Frio — Chilrão — Fonte (11.3km/7mi; 2h37min). Grade and notes as for main walk, but omit the climb to Madrinha.

The *serras* which make up the most northerly part of Algarve are generally dull and monotonous. Their schistose composition generates an acid soil which supports a uniform *matos* consisting mainly of gum cistus, *Cistus ladanifer*. But the Serra de Monchique is altogether different. Its greater height gives it an imposing presence, and its granite composition favours a more varied and interesting flora. This area provides the most demanding walking in Algarve, and we have put together a selection of five walks which explore all facets of this intriguing and very different region.

After first climbing the nearby summit of Madrinha

(802m/2650ft) to enjoy the views, this walk then descends its western slopes, to visit two small villages before circling back by a different route. It starts from the viewpoint near the top of Foia signposted 'Fonte/Mira-douro'. It's not unusual to find one or two locals here, offering to sell home-made produce to passers-by. Honey and *medronho*, a spirit made

Pé do Frio — just a loose scattering of farm houses

from the fruit of the strawberry tree (see page 73 for more information), are usually on offer. **Start out** from the centre of the *miradouro* by following the waymarked path, initially heading down and away from the road. Almost immediately the path swings right to head towards the nearby peak of Madrinha, which is easily distinguished by its trig point. Keep an eye open for the red and yellow waymarks which are not always so obvious. At the fork reached in **4min** go left, but ignore the next two left turns in the following minute, to keep heading towards Madrinha. Keep straight ahead at the cross-paths reached in **7min**, to meet a 'T' of paths, where you go right. The waymarked route now leads between two large ponds (**9min**), to arrive beneath Madrinha. Here the path broadens to become a woodland track. Although the summit seems close by, up on the right, the access point to it is much further around the mountain. Stay with the track and look for the waymarked path off left, reached in **16min**. Clear views over the hills rolling and undulating in timeless motion down to the coast demand attention as you traverse this section. Portimão and Lagos are the two major coastal towns which are in view on a fine day.

On meeting a rough track in **22min**, turn right to start the diversion up to the summit (but turn left for Short walk 2). A clearing is soon reached, where you skirt to the left, to pick up a grassy two-wheeled track. This leads to and continues across a major track (**25min**), then rises towards a clump of pines (**29min**). Another small clearing and a track lie not far ahead; cross them, to follow a still-rising path. Turn right on joining the rough track a minute later; it leads to the summit (**34min**), marked by a trig point and a fire watch station. This is one of the finest viewpoints in the region and, given a clear day, it is possible to pick out a whole host of landmarks stretching the full breadth of Algarve.

Retrace your steps back to the start of the summit diversion, which is reached again in **45min**. Continue down the track through a eucalyptus plantation. Ignore the woodland track joining from the left in **52min**, but go left at the division reached two minutes later. The tracks rejoin shortly, but the left offers easier walking. Keep descending, ignoring all side tracks, with the summit of Picos close by on the left and views to Pé do Frio on the right. A junction with a major track is reached in **1h08min**. This is the new route to Pé do Frio, but the old one is more scenic, so cross the wide track and take the smaller track running diagonally right. Stay right at the fork reached two minutes later, to enjoy good views across the valley to Pé do Frio. Where the main track swings down left (**1h12min**), keep ahead on the lesser track, passing a small house on the right. Citrus groves, never without either fruit or flower, add a new verdure which contrasts sharply with the nearby cork oaks (see photographs on pages 37, 119 and 120). At **1h22min** turn right at the junction to enter the main part of Pé do Frio, which is just a hamlet. Turn left on meeting the main track less than a minute later.

Chilrão soon comes into sight. It too is just a scattering of farm houses and has no shops (**1h42min**). Keep on the main track to pass the village and stay ahead at the junction two minutes later, following the signpost to Portelo da Viuva. Ignore the track joining from the left in **1h46min**, but look for the rough track ascending to the right less than a minute later, at a point where the main track is itself starting to bend away to the right. Slip into low gear as the uphill section now gets underway, with good views on the left. Stay ahead at the diagonal cross-track (**1h57min**). Shade is mostly left behind now, as you head more directly for Foia. A stream passes under the track (**2h02min**); just over a minute later, head right, where a rough track continues ahead. Stay with the track as the route describes almost a U-turn to the right, with a valley and views to Picos on the right. Be sure to keep left in **2h15min**, where a track descends ahead; then, a minute later, go sharp left, staying with the track. From this sharp bend there are some spectacular views, especially the sight of the steep terraces just below Madrinha. You can also see a zigzag of tracks below Foia; this is where our route will eventually take us. There is another sharp turn, this time to the right, in **2h18min**, where a minor track continues ahead.

Terracing brings a neat order and grace to the steep hillsides, as we continue steadily uphill along the main track. There is some shade for a short time as you pass through a eucalyptus wood (**2h34min**). As you leave the wood, it becomes clear that you are walking a horseshoe circuit around the valley down to your right. Pé do Frio and Chilrão can both be seen below. Soon there is a fork in the track (**2h51min**), where you keep up to the left. All along this section there are fine views down over old terraces and farm clusters. The track rises to join the surfaced road (**2h58min**), where you turn right to arrive back at the *miradouro* two minutes later.

5 MONCHIQUE • FOIA • MONCHIQUE

Distance: 11.2km/7mi; 2h40min   **See map pages 72-73**

Grade: moderate. Monchique is situated at an elevation of around 400m/1312ft, which still leaves 500m/1640ft of climbing before you reach the top of Foia. Although the route is fairly direct, the going is rarely very steep, which makes the walk less strenuous than it might appear.

Equipment: sturdy shoes or boots, long-sleeved shirt, long trousers, sunglasses, suncream, cardigan, raingear, picnic, water

How to get there: 🚍 by bus from Portimão to Monchique (Timetable 3). Journey time 55min. 🚗 by car: park in Monchique's main square or at the viewpoint on the right, as you enter the square.
To return: 🚍 bus back to Portimão (Timetable 3), or car

Short walks

1 Monchique — Franciscan convent — Monchique (1.6km/1mi; 21min; easy; no special equipment required). Follows the main walk to the ruins of the 17th-century convent; return the same way.

2 Foia to Monchique (5.6km/3.5mi;1h20min). Same grade and equipment as main walk. Take a taxi for the 8km journey from Monchique to the top of Foia and use the notes (in reverse) to walk back down. Start out from the car park, by heading down to the nearest cluster of aerials and dishes, to find the track leading off to the left.

At 902m/2960ft, Foia is the highest peak in Algarve, but the summit — adorned as it is with clusters of radio and television masts, a concrete obelisk, restaurant and gift shops — is not especially pretty. However, the views are truly panoramic and, should you be fortunate to choose a clear day, you can see Sagres on the southern side and out to Cape St Vincent — one of the most westerly tips of mainland Europe; to the north the mountain ranges south of Lisbon are visible. Monchique itself seems to offer little of interest as you arrive in the main square, but you will discover the real character of the place in the narrow streets where the walk begins.

The walk starts from the main square, Largo 5th Outubro, where you alight from the bus. Leave the square from the top right-hand corner from where you entered, along the narrow cobbled street to the right called Rua de Porto Funda. In less than a minute turn left into a narrow alley (Travessa das Guerreiras) and climb the shallow steps to cross a narrow street (**2min**) and continue upwards. At the next junction, reached in less than a minute, keep to the right of the café on the corner opposite and swing left in front of the ruined Colegio de Santa Catarina. Still climbing, swing right in **4min** and continue in a steep ascent out of Monchique. In **6min**, where the road goes down right, keep ahead to join an old trail which leads past a water pumping station and a shrine on the wall, both on the left. Good views soon open up back

69

towards Monchique to the left and across to Picota on the right, where you can see the trig point and the fire watch tower (both visited in Walk 8). Ignore another old trail which sweeps off to the right (**9min**) and continue ahead to the ruined Franciscan convent of Nossa Senhora de Desterro (1623).

Go right as you reach the convent (**11min**), or after you have finished exploring it, to continue around to the back; then take a path which leads directly away through the woodland. Cork oaks provide shade as you follow the path around the contour of the hill, perhaps just rising a little before meeting an old trail (**13min**). Turn left now to leave the oak woodland and start in a steeper ascent. The trail swings left and divides shortly afterwards (**17min**); go right here and meet a broad stabilised track in less than a minute, where you turn left. But be sure to turn right almost immediately, onto a rough track. Just about a minute up this track (**19min**), take the path which leads off to the left. Woodlands shade the way as you climb steadily, to emerge on another track in **22min**; here turn right.

Scents of pine and eucalyptus mingle as you tread softly on the carpet of forest litter. On meeting the next track (**27min**), turn left. A short steep descent takes you down to a major track and a right turn three minutes later.

As you continue left, the track crosses a stream tumbling down towards Monchique. When the main track swings sharp right (**36min**), keep ahead on a narrow woodland track and prepare for the steeper ascent to come. Sunlight filtering through the eucalyptus canopy provides dappled shade as you climb. Ignore the track joining from the left in **39min** and the diagonal cross-tracks five minutes later.

Foia, easily distinguished by its cluster of aerials, comes into view as you emerge from the woodland. From here the track sweeps sharply to the right, and you can see the large reservoir, Barragem da Bravura, to the southwest. Stay with the track in its winding ascent, to pass a farm-house on the left (**51min**), as you again swing sharply right. The climbing eases from this point and, with only 200m/650ft to ascend, you start to get a flavour of the views from the summit. Patchy woodland, including some chestnut, provides a little shade from time to time, but where the views are open there is as much interest in the immediate landscape shown below as in the distant views. Terraces woven into steep hillsides suggest a sleep of centuries, isolated farms shimmer in the sun, and the sense of tranquillity is enhanced by the sound of distant cow bells. The summit is reached in **1h18min**. Continue to the right to find the shops, restaurant and car parking area.

Once refreshed, return the same way.

The open countryside below Foia. Some of the flora you can expect to see on this walk in early season are the small funnel-shaped lilac flowers of Romulea bulboco-dium, blue Scilla monophyllos — a plant easily distinguished by its single leaf, and the broad-leaved Epipactis helleborine.

In Monchique itself, it is interesting to see how bright yellow Bermuda buttercups manage to colonise even the walls of the narrow streets (see photograph page 38).

6 MONCHIQUE TO CALDAS DE MONCHIQUE

Distance: 6.4km/4mi; 1h23min

Grade: easy — mostly on tracks which are good underfoot

Equipment: sturdy shoes or boots, long-sleeved shirt, shorts or long trousers, sunglasses, suncream, cardigan, raingear, picnic, water

How to get there: 🚌 bus from Portimão to Monchique (Timetable 3). Journey time 55min.

To return: 🚌 bus from Caldas de Monchique to Portimão (Timetable 3). Journey time 40min.

Alternative walk: Monchique to Caldas (8.5km/5.3mi; 2h05min; same grade and equipment). The main walk joins circular Walk 7 and takes the shorter route back to Caldas. For this longer alternative walk, you can go the other way around the circle, when you join Walk 7 at the 1h20min point. Turn right here and follow the notes for Walk 7 in reverse.

This walk usefully connects Monchique and Caldas de Monchique with the very minimum of road walking. If you haven't time to do walks based on both Monchique and Caldas, then this allows you to see both places. You could also do Walk 8, for example so that you could enjoy Monchique and the heights of Picota, and then end up

relaxing in the square at Caldas, the small and interesting spa town shown on page 36 and described in Walk 7. The route leads through a cultivated valley where almond blossom tints the spring landscape in the palest shades of pink, and later the oranges and lemons provide their display which fills the air with delightful fragrance. Olives and figs are around too, but another especially valuable fruit grows here, which passes unnoticed by many visitors. This is the fruit of the strawberry tree, *Arbutus unedo*. It is particularly common near Caldas:

As the name indicates, you eat only one! The fruits themselves are unpalatable, but they make a splendid *aguardente*, a firewater called *medronho*. The tree flowers in September and October, and it is at this time that the previous year's fruit starts to ripen and really resembles a strawberry. Only then is it ready for collection. The fruit is fermented in wooden barrels to produce alcohol with only enough water to cover the mass. The natural yeasts already present on the fruit start the fermentation. Mud is used to seal the barrels, with a tube for escaping gases, to protect the alcohol from further conversion. By January the fermentation is usually complete, and it is ready for distillation. This process uses a

specially-designed copper kettle, which is heated over a wood fire. A medium-sized kettle will handle about 100 kilos of the fermented brew, but the mass needs to be stirred by hand to prevent burning, until it is necessary to fit the tubes ready for distillation. A slow and steady distillation rate gives the best results and produces *medronho* which is about 90% proof. Your visit to Algarve will not be complete without sampling some *medronho* at one of the bars in Caldas ....

Leave Monchique on the road to Portimão. In **3min** turn left onto a track between the buildings and, a minute later, at a T-junction opposite a water tap, turn right onto a cobbled track. Keep around to the right in **6min**, following a path by a wall on the right, to skirt a new building on the left. Go down and round to the right on meeting a cross-path two minutes later and, when you meet the stream (**9min**), keep it on your right. Follow a cobbled path down towards the bottom of the valley. At a junction with a track (**11min**), turn right, to pass a house on the right. The track leads out of the valley, up to the Alferce road (**15min**).

Head for the triangle in the centre of the road, at the junction with the nearby Monchique/Portimão road. Cross over and go left towards the petrol station, on the section of road lined with giant *platanos* trees. Turn right into the entrance to the petrol station (**16min**), but pass between the petrol station on the left and a restaurant on the right. Immediately the road runs into track. Ignore the track off right, less than two minutes later, and continue along the right-hand side of a wide cultivated valley. Stay with the main track as you descend gently, enjoying views over citrus orchards and olive groves, with occasional glimpses of the Picota summit over to the left. Pass a school on the left (**37min**) and continue round to the Marmelete road (**39min**). Cross over onto the track directly opposite and follow the main track around to the left, where a smaller one keeps ahead. Soon pass a cluster of houses and start to descend to a fork (**44min**), where you keep around to the right. As you round the bend less than two minutes later, take the path off to the left. From here follow the notes for Walk 7 (from the 1h20min-point) to continue to Caldas.

7 CALDAS DE MONCHIQUE CIRCUIT

Distance: 8.0km/5mi; 2h See map pages 72-73

Grade: easy-moderate. There is some climbing involved, but not too much. Some of the tracks used are stony and difficult underfoot.

Equipment: sturdy shoes or boots, long-sleeved shirt, long trousers, sunglasses, suncream, cardigan, raingear, picnic, water

How to get there and return: 🚌 bus from Portimão to Caldas de Monchique (Timetable 3). Journey time 40min. 🚗 by car: Approaching from Portimão, take the second road signposted to Caldas (the first does not allow car access to the centre). Park in the area provided.

Short walk: Caldas — watermill — Caldas (2.0km/1.25mi; 30min; easy; no special equipment required). Follow the notes for the main walk as far as the lovely old watermill on the stream and return the same way.

Caldas de Monchique, tucked away in a thickly-wooded valley below a crook in the main road, reveals little of itself as you drive up to Monchique. You might think that there is nothing to see, but this delightful old spa town dates back to Roman times, and its waters reputedly cure a fair range of ailments. The locals clearly have faith; they queue all day long to fill their water bottles from the weakly-flowing fountain. The umbrella-shaded tables in the town square, shown on page 36, create a lovely ambience to sample the *medronho* (see page 73).

Start the walk from the car park, by keeping right, to follow the exit road out of Caldas. The fountain is soon passed on the left and, shortly afterwards, the hospital (**3min**), followed by the water bottling plant, also on the left. In **5min**, just before you reach the bus shelter on the right (opposite a picnic area), turn right down cobbled steps to the riverside. The path continues along the river through a narrow leafy valley with more picnic areas. Cross the bridge (**7min**) to continue along the river. Stay ahead in **11min**, as you rise to join a track coming from the left. A minute later, take the path sharp right, down to the old watermill by the bridge shown overleaf.

Return to the track (**14min**) and continue in the same direction. The views become more open as you follow the track to the right, where it describes a horseshoe to cross the river and heads back up the other side of the valley. Shortly after passing a farmhouse on the right (**20min**), the good track effectively runs out, but continue ahead on the extremely rough and partly overgrown track. It is a steep climb from here, but the reward is more open views back to Caldas — and to Foia over to the right. The strawberry tree (see page 73) is common along here. With so many loose stones, the downhill sections on this track need special attention. Keep ahead as you join another rough track leading in from the left (**31min**). Stay ahead on this track, through eucalyptus plantations, and ignore tracks joining from the left. In **51min**, as you climb to the highest point of the walk, you enter a region of cultivation.

Pines and eucalyptus soon give way to olive groves on the left and figs on the right. The now-walled track is easier walking. Ignore the track joining from the right (**56min**) and keep ahead when you meet tracks running in from the left (one and two minutes later). Views open up over the valley to the right, where you can see the Monchique/Portimão road. Stay ahead, ignoring the track on the left (**1h05min**), as the main track swings right, but look for a smaller track — also walled-in — on the right (**1h11min**). This leads initially through a small woodland of cork oak towards a house. Where the track divides, stay ahead to pass in front of the house on the left (**1h13min**). Immediately beyond it, as the track swings around to the right, join the wide path running ahead. Keep left at the fork a minute later, to descend towards the stream. Turn right (**1h16min**) to cross the stream on good stepping stones and follow the path through the woodland, staying ahead on the lesser path less than a minute later, where the main path sweeps away to the left. Ignore the crossing path, to emerge alongside a house at the end of a track (**1h18min**). Turn left here and look for a path off right two minutes later (**1h20min**), leading towards a small house (Walk 6 joins here). Stay with this good path, keeping around to the right (before reaching the house on the left), to skirt around and descend a largely cultivated valley on the left. Pass a small concrete building on the right, before crossing the stream at the bottom of the valley. In **1h24min** meet a 'T' of paths. Turn left and continue as the path broadens to a rough track and leads within a minute into a builder's storage area, where you turn left. Keep ahead to cross over another track (**1h26min**) and, a minute later, as you converge on a major stabilised track, cross it to the right, to join a stony track running parallel to the main Monchique road which you can see over left.

This route now heads in a southerly direction, more or less following the line of the road. Stay left at the fork encountered in **1h33min** and climb up to join another track almost immediately, where you keep right. Ignore side tracks for a time, until you climb to the main road (**1h39min**). Don't join the road; bear right onto a track by the road, which leads straight away into a cleared area. Cross it by skirting around the left edge, until you reach the old track (**1h41min**), which continues through light woodland of pine, cork oak and strawberry trees. Turn right as you run into a minor woodland track a minute later, and sharp right as you meet a major track almost immediately. This leads on a curving descent to the left. Soon (**1h45min**) this track, now starting to look less significant, swings sharply right (down to a farm); here a path left goes back to the road. Keep ahead to join a grassy path, which soon becomes stronger. It wanders through the woods just below road level, but then rises up to join it (**1h48min**). Take care on the road, as you continue downhill. In three minutes, where the road bends left, turn right, taking the left-hand track heading down towards Caldas — it comes into view as you reach the first corner. Stay with the main track; the track going ahead (**1h53min**) also returns to Caldas, but is a slightly longer route. As the track runs out (**1h56min**), continue ahead on a path which curves right and down stone steps. Swing left to pass in front of a house and join a track back to the centre.

This bridge by the river is met some 12 minutes into the walk. There are many picnic areas in the woodlands around Caldas; this photograph was taken not far beyond the setting for Picnic 7.

8 MONCHIQUE — PICOTA CIRCUIT

Distance : 9.0km/5.6mi; 2h35mi   See map pages 72-73

Grade: moderate. The ascent of 400m/1312ft is mostly gradual and the footpaths and tracks used are mainly good underfoot.

Equipment: sturdy shoes or boots, long-sleeved shirt, long trousers, sunglasses, suncream, cardigan, raingear, picnic, water

How to get there: 🚌 bus from Portimão to Monchique (Timetable 3). Journey time 55min.

To return: 🚌 bus from Monchique to Portimão (Timetable 3)

Shorter walk: Monchique — Picota — Monchique (6.6km/4mi; 2h; same grade, equipment). Do the main walk (in reverse) from the Alferce road, to go to Picota (mostly on woodland track); return the same way.

Picota is the twin of Foia, peaking a little lower (at 774m/2540ft). Monchique nestles in the valley between the two. Picota provides interesting walking, with the added bonus of tranquillity on the summit. Botanically it is possibly the more interesting mountain, although the eucalyptus plantations to its north do nothing to help in this respect, since their thirsty roots denature the soil.

Start the walk from the main square in Monchique by heading out along the Lisbon road, passing the fish market on the right. Take the right fork (**5min**), signposted 'Cruz dos Madeiros', to descend a narrow street which soon becomes cobbled. Keep around to the right as you approach this hamlet two minutes later, and enjoy the shade of this leafy lane which runs into a track as you approach a fork (**8min**). Go down to the right through the cork oak woods, catching glimpses of terraces across the valley to the right. Ignore the path that soon comes up on the right but, in **13min**, take the right fork: this starts as a track, but soon becomes a cobbled trail. Cross a dirt track a minute

From about the 30min-point in the walk, there are fine views across the valley to Monchique, nestling below the lower slopes of Foia

later, to continue down towards the valley floor. Turn left at a junction reached three minutes later, along the main trail running parallel to the river below right. When you meet the bend of a track (**18min**), go down right, to cross the bridge over the river. Almost immediately past the bridge, turn left into a walled track, crossing a stream. The track runs only to a house (**21min**), but a footpath continues along the right-hand side of it. This quickly leads to a fork, where you keep right to continue alongside a wall. Soon back in a walled-in path, you can enjoy views over this fertile and well-cultivated valley, where the orange trees add a splash of colour throughout winter and spring.

In **25min**, after rising steeply and passing a farm on the left, the path runs into a rough dirt road, where you keep ahead to join a stabilised track coming in from the right less than a minute later. Keep right at the fork reached almost immediately, to climb back into cork oak woodland; then stay with the main track as it swings right (**30min**). Looking back from here there are fine views of Monchique across the valley, nestling against the lower slopes of Foia. The cork collection point shown on page 120 is passed just before reaching a cross-track (**35min**); turn right here, up an old track, passing a farm on the left. You reach the Alferce road just over two minutes later.

Cross directly over the road, to approach a trail and a path opposite. Take the path on the left; it climbs above the small but steep wooded valley on the right. Turn onto the path leading to the right (**40min**), ignoring the walled-in path which starts ahead. You cross over the head of the valley and a small stream. The path leads left and then right, to pass above a ruin two minutes later, before meeting the bend of a woodland track coming from the right (**44min**). Continue ahead through cork oak and eucalyptus. Follow the track in a steady ascent to the left of the buildings as you approach the next track junction (**48min**). Turn left here, and then turn right almost immediately — just before the farm buildings. Four minutes later, come to a higher track, where you turn right, heading towards a narrow surfaced road and taking in views of Monchique across the valley as you go. Turn left and climb steeply uphill when you reach the road (**54min**), but watch for a footpath off left through the woods in just over a minute. The young eucalyptus plantation provides some shade as you continue on this path in a steady ascent.

A stabilised track is joined in **58min**; turn left. Stay with the main track, following a selection of different coloured waymarks which are used here as directions to isolated homes. Follow the red arrow for the moment, heading right at a fork (**1h04min**); go right again less than a minute later. The woodland becomes more open, to give fine views of Foia. Follow the main track as it swings between buildings (**1h10min**), after which the track degenerates noticeably. Beyond a sharp left-hand bend in the track (**1h13min**), you reach a fork two minutes later: go left on the older track, through the eucalyptus. Meet a track from the right (**1h23min**), where you keep ahead. Very shortly after this junction, as you reach a high point (and before starting to descend), look for an orange arrow on a rock: turn right here, to join a path which is waymarked with orange dots. Turn left as you emerge onto a track (**1h 30min**), now heading for the summit, which comes into view as you pass the track joining from the left four minutes later. The haul up to the summit is quite steep; clamber over the rocks to reach the trig point and fire watch station (**1h40min**). There are fantastic views over towards Foia, where you can see the convent visited in Walk 5. Looking south, the Barragem da Bravura can be seen, as well as Portimão and Lagos on the coast.

Leave the summit on the far side of the watch tower from your first approach, following orange dots. Descend carefully over the granite rocks, heading for a path between the plantations of pine to the left and eucalyptus to the right. Soon after joining this path, in **1h45min**, look for a path off right through the eucalyptus: it is a strong path, soon broadening into a woodland track. Turn right to continue downhill when you meet a major track on a bend (**2h03min**). Come to a narrow surfaced road (**2h12min**) and turn left. In just under five minutes reach the main Alferce road, where you again turn left. On approaching the Monchique/Portimão road junction (**2h21min**), turn sharp right to enter a walled-in track, which leads back in the direction from which you have just arrived, but at a lower level. When the track runs out at a house three minutes later, turn left onto a path, heading for Monchique. There is a stream on the left for a time as you climb this sometimes-cobbled path. Ignore the cross-path (**2h 27min**) and continue to climb — until you meet a wall on the left (two minutes later). Before reaching some new apartments, go up the trail to the left, which soon becomes cobbled. As you come to a tap on the right, turn left onto a track which leads out to the main road (**2h32min**). A right turn here takes you back to the centre of Monchique.

9 SILVES CIRCUIT

Distance: 7.5km/4.7mi; 1h45min

Grade: easy. Not so much climbing is involved, and the tracks and paths used are mostly good underfoot.

Equipment: sturdy shoes or boots, long-sleeved shirt, long trousers, sunglasses, suncream, cardigan, raingear, picnic, water

How to get there and return: 🚌 by bus from Portimão via Lagoa to Silves (Timetables 4 and 5; C & C buses from Portimão; RN buses from Lagoa). Journey time 37min. 🚃 by train to Silves station (Timetable 11), but be warned that the station lies some 2km/1.25mi outside the town. 🚗 by car: Park by the ring road, in the large parking areas provided on the south side of Silves.

Short walk: from Silves to the windmill and return (4.8km/3mi; 1h05min). Follow the main walk for 32 minutes; return the same way.

Silves is a lovely old town situated on the River Arade. Apart from enjoying the ambience of the town square, there are several places of particular interest — including the castle, the cathedral, the museum and the old port area. Legend has it that Silves (or Cylpes, Chelb or Cilves, to use earlier names), was founded on its present site by the Cynetes some one thousand years BC, and since that time it has been occupied by a succession of races from all over Europe and Africa — including the Greeks and later the Romans, around the first century AD. Its subsequent history is turbulent, with bloody battles, times of peace and prosperity, total decline, and devastation by earthquakes. The small museum is worth a visit, to see the coins and ceramics and other relics of these past civilisations and events. It is in the tower of the main gateway, in the old Moorish city walls, just by the main square.

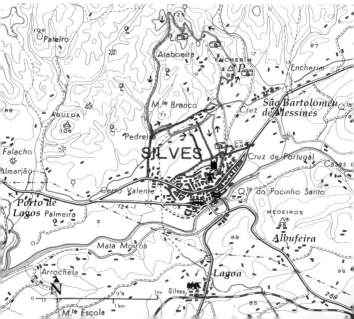

Passing beneath the towering arches of an aqueduct, we approach this windmill above Silves. Orange trees predominate in this tranquil landscape, where the large quaking grass, Briza maxima, flourishes by the side of the road.

It was the Arabs who left behind the most impressive remains — the castle, the Albarranian Towers, the Almadinna walls, the underground well. The castle enjoyed its heyday under the Moors in the 10th-12th centuries. During that period Silves was an important city, more important even than Lisbon. Situated in a rich agricultural region, it boasted opulent buildings, a thriving port, and markets. The decline began in 1189, when Silves came under siege as part of the third crusade to oust the infidels from Algarve and spread Christianity. The slow decline of the city was finally completed by the earthquake of 1755, when the castle, the tower, and the town hall were badly damaged, and Silves ceased to be the capital of Algarve. Many of the walls are still intact, as is the underground well — romantically named 'Cisterna da Moura Encantada' (the enchanted Moorish girl's well).

You can enjoy all this at your leisure. At present there is no charge to enter the castle. If you look northeast as you walk the castle walls, you can see the old windmill shown above, perched on a hilltop. This lies on our route and is the destination of the Short walk. The cathedral, which you pass on the way to the castle, was built in Gothic style by King Afonso X during the last part of the 13th century. It became the cathedral of Algarve until, in the middle of the 16th century, the seat of the bishop was removed to Faro. Little is known about the fate of the silver treasures or the large library which were believed to have existed.

If you park in the car park or arrive by train, follow the signs for 'Câmera' (Town Hall), to direct you up to the main square. **Start the walk** from here, by heading out through the high arched gateway of the tower, following signs to 'Castelo/Sé.' The cathedral (*Sé*) is passed on the right after three minutes; just beyond it lies a junction where the walk continues to the right. (But first cross the junction and then go right to visit the castle, before returning to this point to continue — times *not* included below.) At the next junction, a minute later, keep down left. Immediately on the right is an acacia-shaded picnic area and, across the road below it, are terraces and a children's play area. Keep ahead at the next junction (**5min**), now passing beneath the walls of the castle on the left. As you reach a crossroads (**9min**), turn left and then immediately right, to join a track which leads to the right of an extensive fenced-off orange grove. Looking back, there are some especially fine views of Silves castle to be enjoyed, while over to the right there's an area of wetland complete with bulrushes.

As you approach a smallholding (**15min**), keep left on a footpath which rises immediately to meet an irrigation canal. Cross the narrow concrete footbridge and turn right on the path alongside the canal. In **16min** the path leads away to the left, towards a group of houses. As you reach them, less than two minutes later, turn left to join a narrow surfaced road; then soon leave it by turning sharp right on a track. Now you are heading towards the windmill, which is clearly in sight. At the track junction reached in **20min**, turn left and continue around to the right, heading momentarily back towards Silves and passing under the towering arches of the aqueduct. At the junction of tracks just beyond the aqueduct (**23min**), turn sharp left to pass once again beneath the towering arches, and stay right at the fork encountered almost immediately. Turn right off the main track onto a lesser track in **27min**, to keep the windmill now up to the left. As you reach the brow of the hill less than two minutes later, turn left up a two-wheeled track, passing in front of a white building on the right. Follow the track around to the left on arriving at the farm, to head straight up to the windmill (**32min**). There is a superb panorama over rolling *matos*-covered hills, with cultivated valleys and an excellent view of Silves. Portimão is visible on the seaward side, and the hills of the Serra de Monchique to the north. Close at hand, sticky-leaved cistus, *Cistus ladanifer*, and lavender, *Lavandula stoechas*, dominate in the dense vegetation; the green-winged orchid, *Orchis morio*, also finds a foothold.

Leave the windmill to continue along the ridge, with your back to the sea. Follow the path along the spine of the ridge until you join a two-wheeled rough track (**36min**). This reduces to path again as it climbs a little, still staying in the centre of the ridge. Good views open up now towards the Bastos Valley ahead on the right. The path divides as you reach the end of the ridge (**41min**); go down left here, following a row of eucalyptus trees and soon passing behind a farm, where you meet a rough track. Turn right, to find that you are walking on a saddle between two valleys, with cultivation down left and *matos* to the right. Keep right on the lower track at the fork reached in **43min**. Go left at a T-junction two minutes later, and continue as the track describes a U-turn to skirt a wooded valley down left. Young eucalyptus provides the immediate scenery, as you descend to meet a crossing of tracks (**51min**), where you turn sharp left to continue downhill. Masses of lavender, olives and carobs now join the eucalyptus as you walk through a valley which is part of a 'keep-fit' exercise circuit. Follow this main track as it winds down the valley, passing exercise area No 3, before joining a wide stabilised track (**1h07min**), where you turn left.

This track leads away from the *matos*-covered hills and back through cultivation towards Silves. The track becomes surfaced road (**1h13min**) as you approach the outskirts of the town, where you keep to the right-hand road on meeting housing. Turn left into a narrow walkway (**1h14min**, just before a huge palm), and follow the walkway around to the right. A surfaced road is met two minutes later. Turn left past houses, cafés and shops, and then turn right down steps (**1h21min**), to join the same irrigation canal that was encountered earlier in the walk. Turn right along the path, to cross the bridge over the canal. Turn left, once over the bridge, and follow the path beside the canal. Cross a surfaced road (**1h26min**) and continue alongside the canal. The circuit is complete when you reach the concrete bridge (**1h30min**); turn down the small path on the right between the giant reeds, to retrace your footsteps back to Silves (**1h45min**).

10 BENAGIL • MARINHA • ALBANDEIRA • SENHORA DA ROCHA • BENAGIL

Distance: 10.8km/6.7mi; 2h40min

Grade: moderate. There is a steep valley, difficult to cross, in the final section of the walk.

Equipment: sturdy shoes or boots, long-sleeved shirt, shorts or long trousers, sunglasses, suncream, swimming costume, cardigan, raingear, picnic, water

How to get there and return: ⇌ only accessible by car. The approach road to Benagil is located on the EN125, 3km east of the Lagoa roundabout and opposite the International School. Although unsigned at the entrance to the road, signs appear at later junctions along this 5km stretch. Don't attempt to drive the final narrow steep descent to the bay and the village beyond; park near the café at the top of the hill.

Short walks: both are easy; equipment as above

1 Benagil — Marinha — Benagil (4.8km/3mi; 1h). Follow the main walk to the very beautiful beach at Marinha. Return the same way.

2 Benagil — Praia de Albandeira — Benagil (8.0km/5mi; 1h40min). Follow the main walk to Praia de Albandeira, a small inlet, where there are café facilties in season. Return the same way.

This is another very picturesque section of the coast which is full of interest — from wild flowers to spectacular beaches. In our view, the beach at Marinha rates as one of the loveliest in Algarve and will probably stay so as long as it remains remote and difficult to get to. It lies in a beautiful natural setting and has the benefit of a small café/bar which is open only in season. The coastline along this section is extremely photogenic (see cover picture and next page), so be sure to carry plenty of film.

Benagil, where the walk starts, is a small fishing village where, if you wander down to the seafront, you will see the colourful fishing boats which are so typically Algarvian. Fish is still an important part of the diet in Portugal, and it figures prominently on the menu in cafés and restaurants. Sardines, or *sardinhas*, are a speciality of the area and, freshly caught and grilled, they bear no relationship to the more familiar tinned product. They are at their best in the

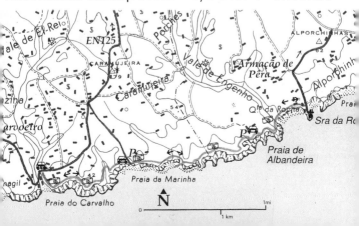

summer season and, traditionally, they are served with boiled potatoes. The finest accompaniment is a chilled bottle of *vinho verde*. The other national fish dish, which is even more popular, is *bacalhau*, dried salted cod. Portuguese fisherman sail out every year, as they have done for the past 400 years, to the Grand Banks off Newfoundland to fish for cod. The catch is salted, sun dried and sold as flat, cardboard-like pieces which you'll see and smell in the supermarkets and markets all over

Portugal. *Bacalhau*, pronounced 'backle-yow', is de-salted and reconstituted by soaking in water and then can be cooked by any one of many hundreds of recipes. In a restaurant which caters primarily for locals there may be several *bacalhau* dishes on offer. Well prepared and cooked in a tasty sauce, it is really delicious ... but if you try it when it is not at its best, then the chances are that it will be your last try!

Start the walk from the café at the top of the hill, by heading down towards the bay. Turn left to mount the steps immediately before the house (**1min**), and notice how the upper steps are cut out of the rock face. Continue along the path, keeping right at the fork, to head towards the coast. From here onwards it becomes a coastal path leading away from Benagil. There is a wealth of wild flowers throughout the spring months, and those we noticed along this stretch included the tassel hyacinth, *Muscari comosum*, the woodcock orchid, *Ophrys sco-lopax* (which is not so common elsewhere in the region), the yellow bee orchid, *Ophrys lutea*, and many of the species already mentioned in Walk 2. Coastline erosion provides some interesting bays and weird formations too, which become especially photogenic later in the walk. In **14min** the path starts to lead inland, to cross an inlet two minutes later. But first there is a diagonal descent to the left, before you go down right to cross the inlet and scramble up the far side, where you find the continuation of the coastal path (**20min**). Now you are at a wonderfully scenic part of the coast, and the views along the cliff, taking in all the incredible rock formations, are quite fantastic (see opposite and cover photograph). Ahead is the car park for Marinha, which you reach in **26min**.

Cross the car park to descend the steps in the far corner and continue along the surfaced path which is stepped in places. If you are stopping for a swim or just for photographs or refreshments, turn left down the steps three minutes later, to reach the superb sandy beach of Praia de Marinha. Otherwise continue along the paved path which leads back to the cliff-top and continues as the coastal path, but now unsurfaced. As you approach a fence (**32min**), beware of the large open sea-worn blowhole, and stay with the path as it skirts the fenced area on the seaward side. Coastal views along this walk include some tantalising sandy beaches which seem only to be

Left: The coast at Marinha (Picnic 10a; see also cover photograph).

accessible by boat. The one seen from here is shown on page 40. An inlet is encountered shortly (**36min**): walk down diagonally left to cross it and, as you rise into a clearing five minutes later, take the very rough track which leads you back to the cliff-edge. The rugged coastline, layered in stratas of gold and cream, and sculptured into intriguing shapes by the restless energy of the sea, presents endless patterns. Another inlet is reached in **44min**, this time rather shallow. Here the naked man orchid, *Orchis italica*, finds a home amongst the rich flora of this coastal region. Then the larger inlet of Praia de Albandeira is soon reached (**48min**).

Cross in front of the café/bar, climb the steps on the far side, and continue along the coastal path. There are views ahead of Armação de Pêra, which looks like villa-land from this distance ... but the turning point comes before it is reached. There is a deep inlet to cross in **55min**, where an inland detour is required. Then head back to the coast, and watch out for more blow-holes. In **1h02min** a very deep inlet is encountered: this one is only negotiable by footpaths which are difficult in parts. Set off inland, staying at a high level, and ignore the first strong path descending to the right soon encountered. Go down, diagonally right, following the second strong path. This is a steep and awkward descent towards the back of the beach. Reach the bottom in **1h09min** and turn right back towards the sea, to find the continuation of the path rising up the other side. It is a bit of a scramble initially, but soon gets easier, as you climb to cross a small headland (**1h15min**). The superb beach at Senhora da Rocha is fully in view from here, and you pass the steps leading to the beach two minutes later.

Continue past the steps, if you want to visit the Romanesque chapel of Nossa Senhora da Rocha on the headland (turn right at the junction reached in **1h 19min**). Some cafés and restaurants lie to the left of this junction, and Armação de Pêra is 2km further east. But our walk ends here, and we retrace our steps to Benagil.

11 CERRO — PICO ALTO CIRCUIT

Distance: 8.0km/5mi; 2h   **See map page 94; see also photo page 28**

Grade: easy-moderate. Although the trig point on Pico Alto stands at an elevation of 276m/905ft, Cerro itself lies on almost the same contour, which means that there is very little climbing to do. The return route, where the footpaths and tracks are sometimes stony, is less easy.

Equipment: sturdy shoes or boots, long-sleeved shirt, long trousers, sunglasses, suncream, cardigan, raingear, picnic, water

How to get there and return: ⛟ only accessible by car. Cerro lies 3.6km northwest of Alte. Approaching along the EN124, turn north into Alte on the more westerly of the two entry roads, and turn left, following the sign to Santa Magarida almost immediately. Turn left again in the centre of Santa Margarida, then park at the viewpoint reached 0.8km later.

Short walks: Both are easy and use equipment as above.

1   Cerro — Pico Alto village — Cerro (6.0km/3.75mi; 1h22min). Omit the diversion to the summit. Follow the walk as far as Pico Alto but, at the 30min-point, turn left down the track, instead of entering the village. Now follow the main walk from the 1h08min-point, to return.

2   Cerro — Pico Alto — Cerro (6.8km/4.25mi; 1h40min). Follow the main walk as far as the trig point on Pico Alto; return the same way.

C erro and Pico Alto, like the villages of Alte and Pena, lie in the Barrocal region of Algarve. The Barrocal is a lens-shaped area of limestone which stretches from Cape St Vincent in the west, reaching its widest around the centre of Algarve, about 20km/12.5mi wide, before tapering out somewhere near Tavira. The limestones are

The villagers in the hamlets we pass en route make a living from the land, and you can see the impact of generations of labourers on the environment, when you return through this beautiful valley.

From the summit of Pico Alto, the views are really rewarding, with a fine panorama embracing Armação de Pêra on the coast, Messines ahead, and the hills of the Serra de Monchique more inland. Around your feet there are yet more orchids, and one of particular interest here is the mirror orchid — or rather a special form of it, in which the lip of the flower has become elongated to resemble an insect. It is Ophrys speculum ssp lusitanica. This photograph was taken looking north from the peak.

dolomites and marls which are seen as whitish rocks, often weathering to dull grey. These are best observed in the scrub-covered ridges which form crests running parallel with the coast — as here on Pico Alto — or, better still, in Walk 14 (Rocha da Pena; photograph page 101). The rich red *terra rossa* soil in the valleys between the ridges is highly fertile, and it is these areas which form the garden of Algarve. Orchards abound, and the crops include orange, fig, almond and carob. The almonds are at their most spectacular in January and February when massed in flower. When their delicate white and pale pink flowers are sprinkled randomly across the valleys it is easy to see why they are sometimes called 'Algarvian snow.'

The plants give a good clue to the various distinct geological regions of Algarve, and the Barrocal provides the richest and most interesting flora. Many flowers typical of the region are seen on this walk, including wild jasmine, *Jasminum fruticans*, orchids, and the striking *Scilla peruviana*. Even the scrub (*matos*) is characteristic, but there are more details of this in Walk 14. This walk leads through some timeless hamlets and a landscape created by generations of farmers living off the land.

Start the walk from the viewpoint, by heading along

the surfaced road towards the first houses of Cerro, which you can see close by. There is a café/bar on the right (**3min**), but most of the village of Cerro is by-passed. Keep ahead, ignoring the road down right (**6min**), and stay ahead where the road runs into track a minute later. For spring walkers there is a wealth of wild flowers to enjoy along this section, including the red peony (*Paeonia broteroi*), the large blue scilla (*Scilla peruviana*), some fine specimens of the man orchid, *Aceras anthropophorum* (its slender spikes are easily overlooked), and the yellow anemone, *Anemone palmata*. Continue along this high-level track, occasionally passing small houses. Note the track joining from the left in **15min**; it is used on the return. Carob trees line the route, while over to the left areas of scrub have been cleared for new orange groves. The houses of Pico Alto soon come into view, and the hamlet is reached in **30min**. The track divides at the hamlet, and the left division is the return route after the climb to the summit of Pico Alto. Continue ahead to enter Pico Alto, and ignore the track joining immediately from the right. Turn right in **31min**, before reaching a large palm tree, to join a path leading between the first and the second house. Keep left at the fork encountered straight away — and notice here the yellow jasmine and the muscari-like *Bellavia hackelii* which is common around here. At the next fork (**33min**), keep right and stay with the main path, as another soon joins from the right. Soon you overlook a large valley down on the right. Stay left uphill at a fork (**35min**), to continue enjoying superb views of the rolling hills inland. As you rise up a little and swing left towards the sea (**40min**), you can catch a momentary glimpse of the trig point ahead. (It helps with the final navigation if you do manage to see it.) As you swing left here, cross the open field diagonally, passing by the spreading carob tree in the centre. There is no longer a strong path, just a variety of animal tracks. Go right as you reach the end of the wall just over two minutes later; then continue by keeping the wall on your right initially. The path is not always clear, but it becomes more distinct further along the ridge, when a wall appears on the left and a valley down right. Again the path fades as you cross a cleared area, but keep following the wall on the left, until the trig point comes almost unexpectedly into sight when you are almost upon it (**49min**).

Enjoy the views shown on pages 90-91 and then, when you are ready to return, retrace your steps. Emerge from between the two houses (**1h07min**), then turn left. Turn right on joining the main track at the entrance to the hamlet a minute later, but then go left almost immediately on an old trail. Ignore another old trail joining from the left (**1h11min**; notice here the old village washhouse on the right). The trail now becomes a stony path, as you head first along a cultivated valley on the right and then start to descend into it. As the path swings right (**1h14min**), ignore the start of rough track on the left and, a minute later, turn up to the left to continue on a more gradual descent. Cross a stream, to meet a very rough track on a bend three minutes later, and continue down to the right. The track narrows to a path in the beautiful isolated valley shown on pages 28 and 91. After passing a small reservoir on the right (**1h20min**), keep right at the fork, joining a wider path which leads down to a main track a minute later. Turn left here and continue with the valley floor just down on the right. At a junction (**1h32min**), turn sharp left to start climbing back towards Cerro. There are some fine views down the valley towards Messines, capped by the distant hills of the Serra de Monchique. The track is stony underfoot as you climb to reach the outward track (**1h45min**), where you turn right back to the viewpoint.

12 ALTE • ROCHA DOS SOIDOS • ALTE

Distance: 13.0km/8.1mi; 2h50min

Grade: moderate. There is a climb to the trig point of Rocha dos Soidos at 467m/1530ft, but it is long and steady rather than steep. Some of the paths and tracks used in the walk are very stony underfoot.

Equipment: sturdy shoes or boots, long-sleeved shirt, sunhat, long trousers, sunglasses, cardigan, raingear, picnic, water

How to get there and return: 🚗 only accessible by car. See Car tour 3, page 37, for details of how to get there and where to park.

Shorter walk: Alte circuit (10.8km/6.7mi; 2h30min; moderate). Complete the main walk, but miss out the diversion to the trig point by continuing straight ahead at the fork (1h17min), following the notes from the 1h50min-point.

Short walk: To the first lime oven and back (4.6km/2.9mi; 1h; easy). Follow the main walk for 30 minutes, then return to Alte a different way, by using the notes for the end of the walk (from the 2h22min-point).

This circular walk explores the country to the west and north of Alte. It offers an interesting mix of scenery and contrasts, passing through the natural prickly vegetation typical of the limestone region of Algarve into more pastoral regions of cultivation. Lime ovens dot the way in the first section of the walk. These round structures were once used to burn limestone which produced lime used for building and to whitewash houses.

Start the walk from the centre of Alte by heading to the right of the church, following the 'Fonte' signs. On

Alte is a small Algarvian village with several points of interest. Apart from the waterfalls just below the village, the main attraction is the spring, 'Fonte Grande', where there is a picnic area. An extension of the picnic site, half a kilometre further along the river, is shown here. It is better equipped, with tables, café/bar and restaurant. It also offers car parking. (Picnic 12)

reaching the fountain area after **6min**, continue on the narrow surfaced road to the left, alongside the river. The main picnic area is reached in **12min**. Continue ahead to join the track, as the surfaced road runs out. Carob trees afford some shade beside the river, its banks splashed pink with oleander. (Note the path descending the hillside on the left in **16min**; this is our return route.) Leave the riverside in **19min**, by taking the track which forks up left. Turn left again two minutes later, to follow an old trail enclosed by grey stone walls. Head up through groves of olive and carob trees. Watch out in early spring for the charming yellow jonquil, *Narcissus gaditanus*, which is so miniature that you could easily miss it. The trail reduces to a path just before meeting a cross-path in **28min**, where you turn right. (Note the path joining from the left a minute later — also on our return route.)

Pass an old lime oven on the left (**30min;** the turning point for Short walk 1), the first of several along the walk. Cultivation is left behind now as you head into the *matos*, where the warm air is scented with the perfume of rosemary, *Rosmarinus officinalis*, very abundant in this area. The route is now taking you in a very gradual ascent along the bottom of a densely-vegetated shallow valley. Ignore the path off left in **38min** (just before passing a lime oven

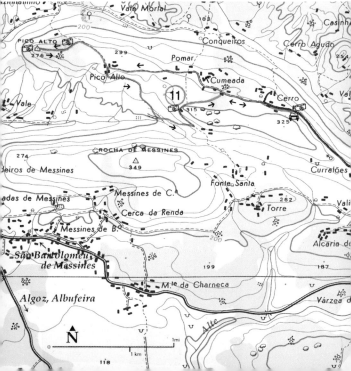

on the right). From this point the path divides and rejoins a number of times so, for simplicity, just keep left at each of the forks, making sure that you still follow the line of the valley. Notice another lime oven on the right in **47min**. The sometimes stony red-earth path starts to lead you out of the valley, and you reach an area clear of vegetation (**54min**), where the path is not so obvious. Keep heading in the same direction, along the right-hand side of the clearing, to quickly pick up an old track which has a green line of cistus shrubs down its centre. Follow its winding course down into the valley ahead, catching views of Rocha da Pena (Walk 14). Head through the middle of the next cleared area (**57min**), and continue as the track swings left and descends more steeply through the *matos*.

Turn sharp left on meeting a rough field track (**1h04min**), as you complete your descent, and continue — now with your back to Rocha da Pena — to head up a small valley, with cultivation on the right. Ignore the path off right a minute later, and continue along this rough track which soon reduces to a path, with a stream on the right. Further over to the right, flower-filled orange groves catch the eye. At **1h12min** you meet a track joining from the right; keep ahead, around to the left of a small bowl of hills at the head of the valley. You meet a section of old

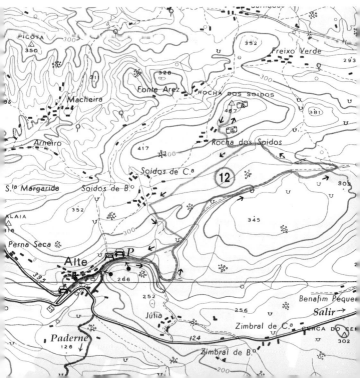

cobbled trail as you climb. Continue to a junction (**1h 17min**), where you take the right-hand fork for the start of the diversion to the trig point on Rocha dos Soidos (but go straight on for Short walk 2). Stay with the main track as it winds up the hill, ignoring all other tracks left or right. Panoramic views open up as you start to rise, with Rocha da Pena over to the right. Keep right as you approach a wall ahead (**1h27min**). When you reach it a minute later, you encounter a walled-in trail leading off left. Ignore this and continue ahead onto a small path which climbs to the trig point. (At the start of this path there is a wall to the left and a small concrete building to the right.) In three minutes the path leads through the wall on the left and climbs terraces, before passing back through the wall again two minutes later. From the trig point (**1h34min**) there are superb views all around. Across the valley, to the north, the village of Sarnadas can be seen and, beyond it, a patchwork of cultivation rolling away into the distance.

Return from the trig point by the same route, until you reach the start of the diversion (**1h50min**); here turn right to continue. The track soon reduces to a trail, stony in parts. It leads back towards Alte, staying level for a time, and overlooking the shallow valley of our outward route. When the trail swings right on approaching a house (**2h07min**), look for the path heading down left on a corner. Follow it down towards a brick building and goat pen, but fork down right a minute later, before reaching them; keep them on your left. Head down and around to the left of a strip of cultivation almost immediately, and keep descending. When more cultivation is reached (**2h10min**), take the left-hand fork, going between two fields at slightly different levels.

Continue on the path beyond the fields; it takes you back towards the bottom of the valley. Ignore the path on the right (**2h14min**); you reach the original outward trail in **2h21min**. Turn right; in a minute you pass the first lime oven encountered on the walk. At the fork (**2h22min**), stay to the right (Short walk 1 joins here), leaving your outward route to return to Alte by a different way. Continue along the stony path; a wall is on the left. Keep left where the path divides (**2h25min**), entering a wooded area. Skirt left to negotiate a fallen tree a minute later, picking up the path again beyond it. Descends gradually at first, but then more steeply. It is rather difficult underfoot before you join the main track (**2h31min**). A right turn here leads back to Alte; you pass the main picnic site just four minutes later.

13 PADERNE • CASTELO • AZENHAL • PADERNE

Distance: 13.8km/8.6mi; 2h47min

Grade: easy-moderate. Some footpaths are followed, but the walk is mainly on tracks which are sometimes stony but mostly good underfoot; uphill sections are few.

Equipment: sturdy shoes or boots, long-sleeved shirt, long trousers, sunglasses, suncream, cardigan, raingear, picnic, water

How to get there: 🚌 bus from Albufeira to Paderne (Timetable 7). Journey time 28min. 🚗 by car: Park on wide main road and join the walk at the 3min-point.

To return: 🚌 bus from Paderne to Albufeira (Timetable 7), or car

Short walks: There is a good variety of interesting shortened versions from which to choose. All of these fall into the easy grade, but require the same equipment as the main walk.

1 Paderne — Castelo — Paderne (6.9km/4.3mi; 1h16min). Follow the main walk as far as the castle and return by the same route.

2 Paderne — Castelo — Albufeira road (7.2km/4.5mi, 1h25min). Follow the main walk to the 1h24min-point, then turn left to the road, for a bus to Albufeira (the stop is almost opposite the end of the track).

3 Paderne — Castelo — Paderne (8.0km/5mi; 1h35min). Follow the main walk to the castle and on to the bridge. Return from the bridge, following the notes for the main walk, but from the 2h03min-point.

4 Paderne circuit (9.4km/5.8mi; 2h). This walk includes the castle, bridge, and café (Azenhal) on the other side of the river. Follow the main walk to reach and cross the bridge. Turn right (instead of left) immediately over the bridge, and follow the footpath along the river to the café. Return by picking up the main walk at the 1h50min-point.

Paderne castle dates back to the time of the Moors. Built on a hill and surrounded on three sides by the River Quarteira, it had a role in the defence of the region during the period of the Arab occupation. The castle was conquered in 1249, during the reign of Don Afonso III, but

Paderne Castle from the bridge over the Quarteira River (Picnic 13)

history does not record whether the battle was fierce and bloody, or whether the castle was damaged. In 1305 it was given by Don Dinis to the Master of the Order of Aviz, Don Lorenco Annes, which suggests that the castle was still in use in that period. Today only the outer walls remain sufficiently intact to remind us of its past grandeur. Much of the interior has been destroyed, although there are still some remains of the chapel dedicated to Our Lady of the Ascension. The nearby high-arched bridge spanning the river is believed to date from an earlier period, from Roman times, when the river was navigable and used to transport materials to and from the sea. It was rebuilt sometime in the middle ages, probably by the Crusaders, and it has survived the ravages of time remarkably well.

Start the walk from the centre of Paderne by heading down the narrow street opposite the clock tower of the church, to pass the post office almost immediately. Keep ahead as you join the main road less than three minutes later, passing a cemetery on the left. In **5min** come to a junction signposted 'Fonte': turn left here and follow this narrow country lane through a region of cultivation to reach a fountain (*fonte*) ten minutes later. From here take the track going off to the left and, almost immediately, bear right at the fork, following the sign 'Castelo'. Straight away the castle comes into view ahead, but there is still some walking through the orange and olive groves to enjoy before you reach it. Stay on the main track until you reach

a fork in **29min**. Here the main track sweeps away to the left and takes a circuitous route up to the castle, but the shorter way is to keep ahead at this junction, on a minor track which leads towards the river. Watch out two minutes later for a path on the left leading up the hillside, and follow this for a short steep climb to the castle (**35min**). If you are a springtime walker, keep an eye open as you climb this hillside for a wealth of orchids, including the lovely *Ophrys bombyliflora* (bumblebee orchid).

From one side of the castle there are open views in the direction of Paderne, but the other side looks down upon the fascinating arched bridge which was part of an old route. We go there next. As you face the castle at the front, leave by a small path which follows the left side of the castle, looking down at first over the old bridge. The path does not descend immediately, but stays at the same level on the flank of this hill, leading upriver and away from the bridge. After three minutes, where the path becomes less obvious (in a cleared area), turn left to pick up the path beyond the clearing. It then swings right and is again easily followed; it leads into a gentle descent, arcing left towards the river. Just before reaching the cultivated area down by the river, veer left towards the riverbank. You will pick up a strong path by the riverside (**41min**). Follow it, with the river on the right, heading downstream towards the bridge. *Arundo donax*, the giant reed, loving the abundant moisture, grows tall by the river, while the dwarf fan palm, *Chamaerops humilis*, is equally at home in the arid ground on the other side of the path.

The bridge is reached in **48min**. Cross it and turn left (the return route enters from the right here, and this is where Short walk 4 turns right). At first continue along the river but, in under a minute, take the path leading uphill to the right, away from the river. It is a steady uphill climb, as you follow this path through an old cultivated area where you climb through the broken wall of a terrace (**57min**) to continue. The path is vague here, but it directs you slightly to the right, where you join a cross-path a minute later and turn left. The path goes around to the right and develops into a lovely old trail leading into a walled-in track which is rough underfoot. Much of the climbing is over by **1h03min** and, as you start to descend a little, there are wider views to enjoy through the almond groves.

The next section of the walk takes you through rural countryside, giving glimpses of views to the north. Turn right when you reach a track junction (**1h08min**), and then go left at the next fork just over a minute later. In **1h12min**, as the main track leaves cultivation to head through the evergreen scrub, turn right onto a very rough track and carry straight on at the cross-tracks a minute later. In **1h14min**, when the track swings away to the right, keep ahead to join an earth track, which soon becomes a walled-in trail. The trackside flora throughout this section is especially colourful in spring. The cheerful yellow *Anemone palmata* is present, as well as the pink flowered *Cistus albidus*, with the occasional orchid like *Ophrys tenthredinifera*, the sawfly orchid. Habitation is soon approached, as the old trail swings between two houses to become a track. Reach a T-junction (**1h23min**) and turn right to meet a stabilised track one minute later (**1h 24min**). Go right here (Short walk 2 goes left and meets the Albufeira/Paderne road almost immediately), following a sign for 'Azenhal'. Azenhal refers to the old watermill that once existed down on the river near the castle.

Follow the wide track back towards the river. Watch out in **1h33min** for a path off right, which cuts off a corner of the track. Then, immediately on rejoining the track a minute later, turn right, up another track, to an old wind-mill (**1h36min**). The machinery is still in place, but take care if you venture inside — it looks in danger of collapsing. Fine views are on offer, with the hills to the north drawing the eye. Return to the track, and turn right. The castle comes into sight ahead (**1h43min**), but a parti-cularly fine view is obtained four minutes later, as you get a bit closer. In **1h48min**, as you near the river, watch for a path descending to the right; it cuts off another corner of the track and within two minutes leads you down close to the old mill (now a bar/café, open only in season).

Turn right to continue past the mill and follow the footpath along the river. The paper-white narcissus, *Nar-cissus papyraceus*, graces the way in early season, and colonies of the Spanish bluebell, *Endymion hispanicus*, revel in the shade of this wooded section of the valley. You reach the bridge in **2h03min**; cross it and turn right on a path which soon becomes a badly-eroded track. Climb to a cross-track (**2h07min**), where you turn left. Stay with the main track as you crest the small hill and start to descend. Keep down to the right when you join the track leading up to the castle (**2h12min**), and ignore the track joining from the right four minutes later. Soon (**2h17min**) a minor track leads off left; here you rejoin your outward route and return to Paderne via the fountain.

14 PENA • ROCHA DA PENA • PENA

Distance: 10.0km/6.2mi; 2h25min

Grade: moderate. Although Rocha da Pena peaks at 479m/1571ft, the starting point lies at 250m/820ft, so there is little climbing. The paths and tracks are generally good, except for the path near the summit, which is somewhat overgrown, and a tricky section down the hillside to the windmill, which requires careful footwork.

Equipment: sturdy shoes or boots, long-sleeved shirt, long trousers, sunhat, sunglasses, suncream, raingear, picnic, water

How to get there and return: ⛟ only accessible by car. See car tour 3, page 36, for details. Park just off the main road, opposite the most easterly of the two entrance roads to Pena, 4km west of Salir.

Short walks

1 Pena circuit (6.4km/4mi; 1h25min; easy-moderate). Follow the main walk but, at the 40min-point, exclude the diversion to the trig point. Pick up the notes again at the 1h40min-point, to complete the walk.

2 Picnic walk (4.4km/2.75mi; 1h; easy). Follow the notes for the first 29min, to the picnic spot shown below, and return the same way.

3 Windmills (4.4km/2.75mi; 1h; easy). Go straight to the windmills and return the same way. At the junction (10min), turn right, and then immediately left, on a stony track which leads up the hillside to the left of the windmills. Turn right on the ridge (28min) to the mills.

This is another walk through the Barrocal limestones of Algarve (see Walk 11 for more details), but only on the diversion to the summit of Rocha da Pena do you encounter the scrub-type vegetation, or *matos*, typical of

Picnic 14: Carob trees offer shade, and there are fine views ahead to Rocha da Pena. Nearby the wild peony, Paeonia broterei, spreads its red flowers around with profusion. Weathered limestone, typical of the Barrocal, is seen in the background.

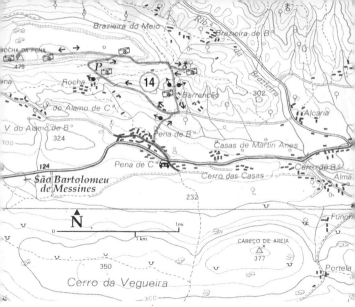

this region. Outside the Barrocal, the *matos* is very different, and some of the characteristic plants are mentioned in Walk 17.

Scrubland is an important type of vegetation in the Mediterranean. But despite many common elements, the scrub is named differently throughout the region. To the east of the Iberian Peninsula, the term *macchie* or *maquis* refers to the tall scrubland, where the shrubs stand about the height of man or more, and *phrygana* or *garrigue* is used for the knee-high, more open scrubland. The Portuguese use one term for both: *matos;* similarly, the Spanish use *mattoral.* The plant communities which make up the *matos* are a good indication of the underlying geology, and are especially easy to 'read' in Algarve, to determine whether you are in the Barrocal region or not. The holly oak, *Quercus coccifera,* whose prickly leaves can make walking in shorts uncomfortable, the shrubby wild olive, *Olea europea,* the wild jasmine, *Jasminium fruticans,* the white small-flowered cistus, *Cistus monspeliensis,* and the dwarf fan palm, *Chamaerops humilis,* are a few of the many plants which reliably indicate the presence of limestone.

From the small village of Pena, this walk leads through one of the many fertile valleys of the region and climbs a ridge from where you can strike out to the trig point. The return route continues along the ridge to visit the two old windmills that are easily visible from Pena, and then drops back down almost directly to the village.

Start the walk from where you park the car, by heading down the side road towards Pena. In **2min** turn right, just before the white-tiled fountain on the right, and head down towards the washhouse. In under a minute, before reaching the washhouse, turn right on a track curving tightly to the right. As it swings around left again, Rocha ('the rock') comes into view ahead, as do some windmills

102

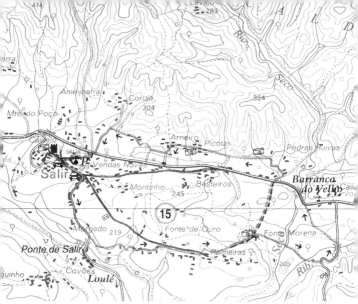

on the skyline. The track now becomes a lovely old trail between olive groves, and you enjoy the tranquillity of rural surrounds for a time. A well on the left is passed (**7min**) and, soon after, the trail rises up to a track (**10min**), where you turn left (but turn right for Short walk 3).

Continue along the track, now with Rocha da Pena up to the right and open views across the valley to the left. (This section of track is due to be surfaced at some time in the future.) At a junction (**23min**) where a very rough track heads uphill on the right (and where ahead you can see a circular fountain built around a carob tree), turn right onto a rough track. The ascent is steep for three minutes, until you pass the point where a track joins from the left. Then the incline lessens, as you enter an area of light woodland. An area shaded by carob trees (**29min**; photograph page 101) enjoys fine views over the farmed valley below; this is a fine picnic setting. Stay on the track as it swings right, to continue under the cliffs of Rocha da Pena, and slip into a gentler pace to counter the steady ascent. Level stretches give some respite, but the open views over to the right are distraction enough to make this section pass quickly. At the top of the hill (**40min**), reach a clearing with a carob tree in the centre, another good picnic setting.

The route up to the trig point on the summit leaves from here, and you will need to return to this point to continue the walk (but go straight on from here, if you are doing Short walk 1). Look for the path leaving the clearing, immediately to the left of where you came in, and follow it. It takes you back along the top of the ridge, through the *matos.* There are places where the path is confused with other animal tracks, so always stay along the south edge of the ridge, looking towards your upward route.

In **50min**, as you reach a bank of stones which extends across the ridge, stay to the extreme left-hand edge, to negotiate your way around it. Looking ahead, pick out the cleared area below the final rise to the summit, and use this as a navigational aid — aim for the left-hand edge. There is a dip in the land as you pass the bank of stones; from here continue ahead, always following the left side of the ridge, until the cleared area is reached (**1h01min**). Cross the field diagonally to its right-hand corner, to find the path continuing towards the summit a minute later. The *matos* is thick and tall here, and you will need to push your way through, following a narrow path, until the next clearing is reached two minutes later. A path to the summit leaves the clearing to the left; it is a little easier to follow, but it is not direct. At first it leads beyond and below the trig point, which you still cannot see clearly through the dense vegetation; then it swings around to the south, to rise onto a rocky ridge. From here you turn left to reach the top (**1h10min**) with its commanding views.

Follow the same route back. Find the minor track beyond the clearing with the carob, and continue with Pena on your right. The track soon reduces to a path; when it forks (**1h44min**), go right and over the edge of the ridge a minute later. The steep diagonal descent is stony underfoot and requires particular care for four minutes, until the path heads more directly towards the windmills. Ignore the path joining from the right and keep ahead. As you near the mills, the path swings around the end of the ridge to the north and meets a rough field track (**1h55min**). Turn right here; you meet a stable track two minutes later and turn left to the windmills in **2h**. One is in a decaying state; the other is closed, so you can see nothing of the workings — but at least you can enjoy some particularly fine views, especially to the north, from this breezy ridge.

From here return along the stabilised track for three minutes, to the point where you first joined it. Look now for a field track descending diagonally left towards Pena. A stream crosses the track as it passes through a dip, before climbing to a ridge (**2h07min**). The track now follows the decline of the ridge between two small reservoirs. Turn right on meeting the main track (**2h14min**), and then go left immediately, to head back to Pena along the outward route. The village shop/bar is by the telephone sign.

15 SALIR CIRCUIT

See map pages 102-103; see also photograph page 32

Distance: 11.0km/6.8mi; 2h10min

Grade: easy-moderate. The walk uses mainly good (although occasionally stony) tracks and paths; there is very little climbing involved.

Equipment: sturdy shoes or boots, shorts or long trousers, long-sleeved shirt, sunhat, suncream, sunglasses, cardigan, raingear, picnic, water

How to get there and return: 🚗 only accessible by car. See details in Car tour 3, page 36. Leave the car on the south side of Salir, in the wide road, just before the junction with the Loulé road.

Shorter walk: 9.2km/5.75mi; 1h50min; same grade and equipment. Follow the main walk initially but, after 38min, do not turn right, but stay ahead on the same track to meet the main road 12 minutes later. Cross directly over, to follow a track leading to the right of a farm, where you rejoin the main walk. Pick up the notes again at the 1h15min-point.

E ven within the confines of the large valley around Salir, there is an unexpected variety in the landscape that can only be appreciated if you are on foot. This walk follows some narrow footpaths, bounded by groves, and broad tracks through wilder regions; it crosses rivers on stepping stones and visits intimate farming communities. We return to the church in the centre of Salir; this is a spectacular viewpoint with an adjacent café/bar and picnic area. We also visit the old castle area (photograph page 32), before heading back to the car.

Start the walk by turning right at the first junction and heading down the Loulé road towards the river and the bridge (Ponte de Salir). In **8min**, just before the bridge, turn left onto a track leading through an area of cultivation. As you approach a farm four minutes later, head first for the entrance to the farmyard, then swing left to take the trail; it soon reduces to a path through olive and carob groves. For

Almond groves around Salir

a moment it looks as though the path finishes at a house, (**15mins**), but turn right along the front of the house, and you will find the continuation. Once over the stream, a minute later, the path leads around to the left and meets a cross-path (**18min**); go right here, and stay ahead as the path winds into a field track. Meet a narrow road a minute later and turn right. You gently ascend a quiet country lane where, if you keep an eye on the roadside vegetation, you might spot the peony, *Paeonia broteroi*, which graces the early months with its elegant red flowers.

As you reach the top of the rise (**24min**), turn left just before the first building on the left. Then turn right just after it, to join a rough walled-in track, and stay on this track through the orange and almond groves shown on page 105. You run into a good stabilised track on a bend four minutes later; keep straight on here. Stay with this slightly elevated track, enjoying the views across the valley to the left. Ignore all side tracks until you meet a junction in **38min** (just after the main track bends left). Here two tracks join from the right. Take the second of these, which is a rough walled-in track leading into a gradual descent through farmed land (but keep straight ahead on the main stabilised track, if you are doing the Shorter walk). Ignore the left fork soon encountered.

The first of two rivers is met in **44min**, and there are just enough stones showing for you to step your way across to continue along the track opposite. This leads to a much stonier river, reached four minutes later. Cross this one by heading diagonally right, and join a walled-in track which climbs up and around to the left, affording views back down over the river before the surfaced road is reached in **53min**. Turn left down the road, cross the bridge four minutes later, and look for a track off left almost immediately. This track leads at first through once-cultivated land, now reverting to *matos*. Head diagonally left after crossing a small stream (**1h03min**), to join a rough field track which swings to the right towards the road and a white house. Pass in front of the house to reach the Salir road in **1h07min**. Turn left downhill along the road and cross the bridge over the Rio Seco. Ignore the first track off right immediately beyond the bridge, but take the second (**1h12min**). After only a minute along this track, turn sharp left to join a rough track which takes you over a small stream and to another track (**1h15min**) coming from a farm on the left (the Shorter walk rejoins here). Now turn right uphill through the cork oaks, towards a small white house. The track swings left just before the house and shortly gives you the first views of the white tower by the church in Salir.

There is a different character to the walk now, as you weave your way back to Salir through a succession of hamlets, taking a course roughly parallel to the main road below left. Ignore tracks right and left, and stay ahead to enjoy views over the picturesque valley on your left — and Rocha da Pena (Walk 14) slightly to the right. Small-holdings are passed from time to time, before you reach a hamlet in **1h35min**. Here you follow the track through the hamlet, as it weaves left at two junctions, heading towards the road. Look for the track going off right within two minutes, to keep you again on a parallel track with the road. Rocha da Pena dominates the views ahead until you reach another track junction (**1h40min**), where you take the uphill route to the right and climb a little before swinging around left to pass through a farmyard three minutes later. Continue along the track as it dips and rises, to pass through another farmyard. At another junction (**1h51min**), turn left to join another track almost straight away; turn left again to head directly towards Salir.

As you join the main road in **1h54min**, turn right and then immediately left, up the road signposted to Salir and Castelo. Turn right just a minute later, to follow a path up towards a higher road, reached in **1h57min**, where you turn right and then left shortly afterwards. Come to the church and the square on the pinnacle of the hill in **2h**. There is a superb panorama from this excellent viewpoint, which you can enjoy at leisure from a seat in the shade — perhaps with a drink from the café. Nearby is a small park area with seating — a pleasant picnic spot, and there is also a children's play park. Our advice is not to picnic here before mid-day since, while the chimes of the church clock are pleasing from a distance, it's more like a sonic boom close by! Leave the square the way you entered it and continue ahead (passing the road by which you arrived) through old Salir, to find the remains of the castle. The second cobbled street on the right (**2h04min**; see photograph page 32), leads you up towards the old ram-parts. You can walk along them by swinging right and continuing around to the left, to complete a circle taking just four minutes, bringing you back to the 2h04min-point, but this time facing the church. Turn right downhill to head back to the car, taking a left turn and then a second left, to get you onto the road where the car is parked.

16 ESTÓI • GUILHIM • FIALHO • ESTÓI

Distance: 15.0km/9.3m; 3h10min

Grade: moderate — mainly on good tracks and paths, with occasional stony and difficult sections. The longest climb is to the top of Guilhim at 313m/1033ft. Some landslips may still exist: see footnote page 113.

Equipment: sturdy shoes or boots, long-sleeved shirt, long trousers, sunhat, sunglasses, suncream, cardigan, raingear, picnic, water

How to get there: 🚌 by bus from Faro to Estói (Warning: not all buses enter Estói; be sure to refer to Timetable 6). Journey time 20min. 🚗 by car: see Car Tour 3. Park on the wide section of road, near the ruins.
To return: 🚌 bus from Estói to Faro (Timetable 6), or by car

Short walks: All are moderate and require equipment as above.

1 Estói — Guilhim — Estói (6.9km/4.3mi; 1h34min). Follow the main walk to the obelisk on the top of Guilhim and to the track below (58min). Go right here and stay on this track, passing close to an old windmill in 10 minutes (the diversion to inspect it adds on 0.8km/0.5mi). Keep on this track, ignoring the track joining from the right in 12 minutes (where Short walk 2 joins). Meet the surfaced road in 17 minutes and then the intersection with the outward route (the 19min-point) six minutes later. Turn left into the trail, to continue back to Estói.

2 Estói — Guilhim — Estói (7.2km/4.5mi; 1h40min). Follow the main walk as far as the obelisk on the top of Guilhim and return the same way, until you reach the end of the track which was first encountered in 41min. From here continue down the track, keeping sharp right on meeting another track 7 minutes later. Stay ahead to meet the surfaced road in 14 minutes and to intersect the outward route (the 19min-point) six minutes later. Turn left into the trail to continue back to Estói.

3 Estói — Guilhim — Estói (9.8km/6.1mi; 2h03min). Follow the main walk to the Bordeira road (1h31min). Then, instead of crossing the bridge, follow the track straight ahead. This leads back (in 20 minutes) to the outward route (the 12min-point). Turn left here, to continue back to Estói. (This short-cut passes a quarry, where it can be very dusty for about five minutes, if you are unlucky enough to catch a passing lorry.)

4 Estói — Guilhim — Faro road (10.1km/6.3mi; 2h11min). Follow the main walk to the Faro road (2h11min), where you can catch a bus.

5 Estói — Fialho — Estói (10.8km/6.7mi; 2h11min). Follow the main walk to the 12min-point. Turn right at this junction and follow the track past a quarry (see 3 above). You join a narrow surfaced road 19 minutes later, where you turn right to cross a bridge and meet the Bordeira road in a minute. From here pick up the main walk (at the 1h31min-point).

E stói has two special points of interest, ruins (Milreu) of the old Roman settlement, Ossanoba, near the start of the walk, and the old palace, the Palacio do Visconde de Estói, at the end. Ossanoba dates back to about the first or second century BC and is thought to have survived until the eighth century AD. It was believed to be a fashionable spa, and the excavations show a bathing complex still with some mosaic work, as well as foundations of houses and the apse of a Roman temple. The 18th-century palace is private property, but the gardens are open to the public and are curious enough to be interesting. This walk leaves

Estói by the bridge over Rio Seco, to head first for the viewpoint on the summit of Guilhim. Taking a northerly route, a broad ridge is followed for a time. This leads you through areas of cultivation, before you eventually curve around to Fialho and cross the Rio Seco again.

Leave the bus at the Roman ruins (closed on Monday) on the outskirts of Estói. **Start the walk** by heading away from Estói, back towards the main Faro/São Bras road, reached in **2min**. Cross it diagonally, to join the track to the right of the surfaced road opposite, and walk straight into rural surroundings where the ubiquitous yellow Bermuda buttercup (see page 38) brightens the way, and where scattered farm houses add interest to this area of cultivation. Keep on the main track as far as the junction reached in **9min**; here stay ahead, as the main track forks away to the right. At the next junction, a minute later, go right, down a narrow walled-in trail which brings you to a major crossroad of tracks (**12min**; Short walk 3 rejoins here, and Short walk 5 continues by turning right). Cross directly over and enter a cobbled walled-in trail, heading in the direction of Guilhim. Keep right towards the hill at the next junction (**15min**). Turn left on meeting a narrow surfaced road (**19min**; Short walks 1 and 2 return this way). Then, almost immediately, go right and continue in a walled-in trail; it soon leads through a hamlet.

In **23min** take the left fork, to follow a trail shaded by carob trees; it winds between farmsteads and becomes more stony underfoot as you start to climb. The views open up to the east, too — towards Olhão and the mound of São Miguel, easily distinguished by the mast on the top. Continue ahead on reaching a crosstrack (**24min**), still following an old trail. When this ends a minute later, keep straight on, to follow a path leading across a field. Stay ahead, towards the sea, following the contour of the hill; there are terraces and a ruined building up on the right. When you cross through a wall (**27min**) and reach a fork soon after, turn right to start the fairly long climb towards the summit. The path, which initially continues to the left of the terrace wall, penetrates the *matos* for much of the way, always rising and never far from the terraces over left. In **30min** you catch a glimpse of the obelisk on the summit of Guilhim, but there is still plenty of climbing to be done. Watch out in **33min**, as the path leads briefly to the right through the disused terraces. Progress through the *matos* is sometimes difficult. In **35min** the path again leads back through the wall on the right and into the old terraces, to continue upwards towards a fringe of white rocks on the

skyline. It weaves out of the terraces and then back into them again two minutes later. The *matos* is left behind for a time, as you continue from here through a grove of carob and pine trees on a more obvious path: it leads into a steep climb over the white rocks and joins a track in **41min**. (Short walk 2 returns from the obelisk to this point before heading down the track.)

As you rest to catch a breath here, you can enjoy extensive views from São Miguel in the east to Faro in the south, encompassing the coastline and the area of plain almost covered in greenhouses. Turn left as you join the track to continue — only to find that the track promptly terminates. A small path leads down left off it; follow this. Fork up right to pass through the wall a minute later, where the path becomes vague for a short distance; then head left along the ridge towards the obelisk. Much of the climbing is over now, and all that remains is to follow the path through the *matos*, to reach the summit in **51min**. It is a fantastic lookout point, with views stretching from the coast in the south to the ring of hills in the north.

With your back to the sea, follow the path which heads, initially, into a steep descent. Keep ahead when the path

This walk passes through a region dotted with picturesque farms, like the one shown here (about 1 hour into the walk). Citrus fruits, olives, almonds, and carobs are commonly grown. The carob is no longer valued for its crop of beans, which was once used to feed the animals. However, these trees are still abundant throughout the area.

runs into a track at a bend (**58min**; but turn right here for Short walk 1), and ignore tracks off right as you continue through the cultivated farmlands shown on the previous page. At a crossing of tracks (**1h05min**) swing right, still following the main track — which now leaves cultivation to head into the *matos*. Cross the surfaced road, five minutes later, and join a wider surfaced road ahead. You catch distant views of Estói as you walk this section. Take the track off right, just as you start to descend (**1h14min**), and follow this rough track, to meet the surfaced road some seven minutes later. Here turn left. Olive and carob trees provide shade from time to time as you wander down this pleasant country lane to meet first the bridge. (The track off right here is used for Short walk 3).

At the Bordeira road (**1h32min**) turn left. Then take the narrow surfaced road on the right, only two minutes later, and, almost immediately, pass a shop on the right. Continue as the road rises steeply, giving views of Estói to the right. In **1h41min**, as the tar runs out, continue on the stony track which soon reveals itself as an old trail. Down right lies a valley which carries the São Bras road, but it is soon evident that there are valleys on both sides, and that our route is following a flat-topped ridge. Where the old trail is overgrown (**1h45min**), continue on the path to the left and cross two fields before rejoining the trail two minutes later, at a junction of paths. Keep ahead here, with a wall on the left; then climb up two banks on the left, before turning right and making for the ruined windmills (**1h50min**). The path leads to the left of the two mills and joins a track almost immediately. Look for a path on the right in two minutes; it soon leads to a crossing path, where you now turn left and head through the *matos* on the top of a ridge towards houses and a track.

The path winds towards the houses, passing close to them, before emerging on a track (**1h55min**), where you turn right. Now there is a clear view of both the obelisk on Guilhim over to the right and the ruined windmills. On reaching a fork that leads either side of a house (**1h58min**), go to the right, down an old track. Take care at the junction reached three minutes later, where the main track swings right, down towards a factory on the main road, and a lesser track joins from the left. Your route is the unlikely field track ahead, leading towards the valley. Ignore the tracks joining from both left and right, and continue as the track widens and becomes stony underfoot. At the 'T' of tracks reached in **2h09min**, follow the main track to the right. With a stream to its left, it leads down to the main Faro/São Bras road in two minutes. (Those doing Short walk 4 can catch a bus back to Faro from here.)

Cross the road to join a track on the far side which leads, in **2h13min**, to an old bridge.* Descend the bank to the right, cross the river on the makeshift wooden structure, and go left, to rejoin the track beyond the old bridge. Ignore the track left almost immediately, and stay down right at the fork in **2h15min**. The track roughly parallels the river, but rises steadily above it. Negotiate the first of the landslips (**2h22min**); a second one is met two minutes later. Down below, regimented orange groves make interesting patterns by the riverside. Keep straight on when, in **2h26min**, you rise to meet a track on a bend: follow a badly-eroded section, leading immediately to another landslip (where the stream crosses). Cross the stream and head up left, to find the continuation of the track which, in spite of the difficulties, is pleasing to walk.

Ignore the track joining from the left in **2h33min**, but take the left fork just a minute later. Estoi comes into view, and soon the way is all descent. The track widens, and there is a sunken section to cross, before an hotel is reached (**2h40min**). Keep to the badly-eroded track to the left of the hotel; it soon leads into a walled-in track passing through the intensely-cultivated environs of Estói. Glimpses of the old palace can be seen before you reach diagonal cross-tracks (**2h51min**). Keep ahead here, with the palace grounds to the left, to pass beneath the bridge joining the palace to the formal gardens two minutes later. The village washhouse and fountain are passed on the left (**2h54min**). Take the first narrow street to the right, just before reaching the small square and, at the next square, continue by keeping to the right, behind the church. This leads to the main square (**2h58min**) and the front of the church, where the bus stops. To reach the palace grounds from here, turn right and you will see the entrance gates. To return to the Roman ruins, set off from the main square with your back to the church and continue along the main road for a further 12 minutes.

*Until 1989 a fine high-arched ancient bridge spanned the river here. Sadly, the exceptionally severe autumn rains of 1989 damaged it to such an extent, that it is extremely doubtful it will ever be restored to its former style. Further on in the walk, the tracks were damaged by landslips (1989/90); sometimes it was necessary to step down as much as a metre (3 feet) in one place — only to climb back up again later. In other places we had to clamber over loose soil. In case these tracks are still not repaired, all the landslip areas are negotiable — with care.

17 SÃO BRAS • TAREJA • VALE DE ESTACAS • SÃO BRAS

Distance: 10.8km/6.7mi; 2h10min

Grade: easy-moderate. There is some climbing involved, through undulating countryside — but nothing excessive. The paths and tracks used are stony and difficult in some places.

Equipment: sturdy shoes or boots, long-sleeved shirt, long trousers, sunglasses, suncream, cardigan, raingear, picnic, water

How to get there: 🚌 by bus from Faro to São Bras (Timetable 6). Journey time 35min. 🚗 by car: park in the wide dual carriageway road (on the route of the walk), leading north from the main square and signposted 'Sanatório'. It is easier to park beyond the shops. On Saturdays, market day, one carriageway is closed, and the other temporarily reverts to two-way traffic.

To return: 🚌 bus from São Bras to Faro (Timetable 6, or car)

Short walks: Both are easy and use equipment as above.

1   São Bras — Tareja — São Bras (6.6km/4.1mi; 1h20min). Follow the main walk *as far as* Tareja. As you emerge onto the surfaced road (35min), turn right and continue ahead along the road, to reach a walled-in track on the right (38min; before the bridge and fountain). Follow the walled-in track and, at the end of the wall on the right less than 2 minutes later, take the path off to the right. Stay right, when the path divides shortly afterwards. This leads through a wall and into an old trail, where you turn left to head up to a crossing track (44min). Turn right now, to link up with the outward route 3 minutes later (the 31min-point in the main walk). Then follow the outward route (in reverse) back to São Bras.

2   São Bras — Tareja — São Bras (8.6km/5.3mi; 1h44min). Follow the main walk *beyond* Tareja, to the point where you meet a track in 53min. Turn right here (instead of left), and follow the track to a surfaced road near a bridge and a fountain down on the left (1h02min). Turn right here and, in just over a minute, turn left into a walled-in track. From here the route is the same as described in Short walk 1 above, so follow those notes from the 38min-point to return to São Bras.

'All roads lead to the river' (55 minutes into the main walk). The setting for Picnic 17 is not far from here.

S ão Bras lies on the edge of the Barrocal, the limestone region. This walk leads through interesting pastoral landscapes to the village of Tareja and continues into a very different region — the schists of the northern *serras*.

Here the acidic soils support a *matos* which is very different from that developed in the limestone regions. Cistus dominate, particularly the large sticky-leaved cistus, *Cistus ladanifer*, which often covers the rolling hills. The large white flowers, sometimes blotched with dark red at the base of the petals, are short-lasting like all cistus and are never produced in sufficient numbers to smother the hillsides in blossom. Cork oaks too are present, as a reminder of an earlier time, when the vegetation consisted largely of oak forest with an undergrowth of cistus. Colour is added by the heaths — the white-flowered tree heather, *Erica lusitanica*, and the pink *Erica australis*, both of which have a prolonged flowering period, and by the dark blue lavender, *Lavandula stoechas*.

Start the walk from where you leave the bus in the main square in São Bras. Follow the 'Sanatório' sign, by heading up the wide dual carriageway road (which is also the location of the Saturday market). In **9min**, at the small roundabout near the end of the dual carriageway, turn right into a wide track and, almost immediately, go left onto a small stony path, with a wall to the left and a stream on the right. A steady ascent begins, as the path leads into a track two minutes later; here you continue ahead, to meet a narrow surfaced road almost immediately. Cross the road to enter a walled-in path which rises to cross another surfaced road (**14min**). Still in steady ascent, take the path opposite which soon swings around to the right into more open countryside. Views to the east here include the mound of São Miguel, with its tall mast.

Keep ahead as the path becomes surfaced underfoot and leads into a descent, as it widens to a narrow road. Turn left as you reach a well, in **20min**, onto a partially-surfaced track, heading towards the brow of a hill. Views open up as you climb here, especially in the direction of São Bras and Faro. From the brow of the hill, reached in **24min**, there are open views towards the sanatorium. Turn right here, into a walled-in track. You meet a surfaced road four minutes later, where you turn right. Enter a walled-in track on the left just a minute later; a farmhouse lies to the right. Soon (**31min**) fork left down a narrow stony path (the return route for both short walks joins from ahead). As you reach some olive groves, the path becomes a field track, running alongside a restaurant to the left. Come to a surfaced road (**35min**) and turn right to enter the village of Tareja, which lies largely up to the left.

Turn left a minute later, onto a path running by the

washhouse, and left again at the road, to head into the village. Walk around right to the T-junction (**37min**) and turn left. From here there is a fine panorama to the north over rolling hills and valleys: it is easy to appreciate the strategic position of the village. Follow the road between the houses, until it swings right and ends a minute later. Continue on the footpath, climbing towards the ridge ahead, with views of *matos*-covered hillsides on the right and the valley already traversed on the left.

As the main path swings right in **39min**, stay ahead on the narrower path leading towards a small plateau on top of the ridge (**40min**). Carpets of *Romulea bulbocodium* display a variety of shades in their small lilac flowers here. Continue over the hill, to meet the corner of a narrow track which can be seen ahead (**41min**). Keep straight on over this very rough surface, to head into the *matos*. Ignore the track coming in from the left (**45min**) and stay ahead, as another track forks off left soon afterwards. The track narrows to a path, stony and difficult underfoot. You descend towards a track (**53min**), where you continue to the left (but turn right for Short walk 2). As you turn left, ignore the track that comes up on the right immediately (it leads off towards the river); stay ahead, passing an old ruin on the right. All roads lead to the river (**55min**; the photograph on page 114 was taken here). If the water is high, go left to find an easier crossing-point higher up, but return to the bank opposite to continue. The river area is a fine picnic spot, brightened by paper-white narcissus and pink oleander.

Once over the river, pass to the right of a ruined watermill and head for another river which joins nearby. Continue left along the riverbank for a moment, until a track is reached, and stay right at the fork shortly encountered. The route follows the line of the river initially, but soon becomes a stiff climb up a two-wheeled track, past the ruins of a house (**59min**). You follow the spine of a ridge through scattered cork oak plantations. Soon after the high point (**1h07min**), the track dips down into a hollow, where another track joins from the right. Take the narrow but distinct path left, heading for a cluster of buildings which can be seen on the road below.

Keep these buildings as your goal where the path is unclear. You follow a small ridge and then descend its left flank towards a meadow. When the path divides (**1h 15min**) stay right, then swing sharp left and, finally, turn right, to walk along a shaded path to the river, reached two minutes later. Cross the river to the left and continue right along the path; it soon becomes track, as you pass behind a cork processing plant. Keep ahead, as a track joins from the left, and meet the surfaced road (**1h20min**).

Turn left, but then leave the road four minutes later (after passing an electricity substation on the left), to take a stony path on the left. It slopes down to a confluence of streams and more paper-white narcissus. Cross the first stream ahead, and go left to cross the second, rising here to join a cross-path, where you continue to the right. This pleasantly-shaded route skirts cultivated land and passes through vineyards. Keep left at a junction (**1h31min**) and continue along a stony trail. Meet a surfaced road a minute later; turn right here, and turn right again almost immediately, into an old walled-in trail. As you rise towards a cluster of houses, where the road is surfaced (**1h35min**), turn left to cross a stone slab over the stream. Follow a path into olive groves. When it divides a minute later (before a house), go right, join the road, and turn left. Ignore the road immediately on the left; keep ahead to the crossroads (**1h42min**), where you turn up right. The cross-track at the top of the rise (**1h46min**) was the 24min-point in your outward route; keep straight on here to return to São Bras.

18 SÃO BRAS • BICO ALTO • SÃO BRAS

Distance: 14.5km/9mi; 3h   **See map pages 116-117**

Grade: moderate. Although there are the normal undulations to cope with, there is no excessive climbing. The footpaths and tracks used are mostly good, but sometimes difficult and stony in places.

Equipment: sturdy shoes or boots, long-sleeved shirt, long trousers, sunglasses, suncream, cardigan, raingear, picnic, water

How to get there and return: See Walk 17, page 114.

Short walks: Both require the same equipment as the main walk.

1   São Bras circuit (7.8km/4.8mi; 1h37min; easy). Follow the main walk for the first 50min, until you reach the junction with a track and a well on the right. Instead of keeping ahead, turn right and pick up the notes from the main walk again (at the 2h11min-point), to return to São Bras.

2   São Bras — Bico Alto — São Bras (11.2km/7mi; 2h20min, easy-moderate). Use the notes for the main walk as far as the surfaced road at Bico Alto (52min). Turn left here and follow the road for six minutes, to reach the point where the main walk rejoins this road (at the 1h37min-point). From here use the notes for the main walk again.

L ike Walk 17, this walk heads out to the north of São Bras through a cultivated landscape, as far as Bico Alto. But the countryside we pass through beyond here is dramatically different, with natural vegetation of cistus and cork oak dominating the surroundings.

The cork oak, *Quercus suber*, is easily identified by its thick layer of corky bark. On most mature trees, you will see that this has been stripped from the lower trunk. The tree needs to be somewhere in the region of 25 to 30 years old before the bark can be stripped for the first time. This 'virgin' bark is prized for its special applications, like the making of life jackets. All the cutting of the bark is done by hand. First a series of horizontal cuts are made; these are then linked by vertical incisions, to allow the bark to be taken off in vertical strips. The exposed trunk is a rich brown colour for a time — until the cambium forms a new layer of cork, and it may be as long as ten years before it is thick enough to crop again. At the processing plant (like the one passed on Walk 17), the sorted strips are allowed to bake in the sun for a further year to allow all the fatty substances to dry from the millions of air-filled cells and passages. After being boiled in water, the now-flexible sheets are flattened and dried again in the sun. At this stage it is ready for grading for its various uses — from shoes to life-buoys, from shuttlecocks to floor tiles and, of course, for corks. The corks for bottles are cut from the sheets parallel to the diameter of the tree. Cork is one of Portugal's major industries and a valuable export. There are photographs of cork trees on pages 37 and 120, as well as opposite.

Start the walk from the square in the centre of São Bras, by following the notes for Walk 17 for the first **31min**. Then, instead of taking the stony path down left, keep ahead to continue along the track. While the lovely spring-flowering *Fritillaria lusitanica* is not common anywhere in Algarve, we did find it alongside this track, almost hidden amongst the shrubs. In **35min**, just as the wall on the right ends, turn left into an old trail (which starts out as a path). After first keeping up to the left, the trail soon descends between walls. Where it becomes overgrown, cut right, through the wall, to continue on a parallel path down through a tree-filled meadow. Turn left on meeting a track (**37min**), and then turn right on coming to a surfaced road a minute later. Stay ahead as you reach a bridge (**38min**; Short walk 17-2 returns from the track on the left via this bridge). Continue along the surfaced road, which shortly peters out into a track. Keep straight on, ignoring the track off left (**42min**) and, as the track swings down left to cross a stream a minute later, turn right, to join

Views over the northern countryside near Bico Alto, seen from behind a cork oak tree (about 1 hour into the walk)

A cork collection point; this one is encountered at the 34min- point in Walk 8. See also photograph on page 37.

a path running along the right bank of the stream. Keep ahead over the diagonal crossing path, as you rise away from the stream in **45min**. An eroded section of path is met very shortly: it can be by-passed by using the field to the right, if you have any problems negotiating it. Turn right on joining a rough track (**47min**), and note that the main walk rejoins from the left at this point on the return route. Keep ahead as you meet an old walled-in trail (**50min**), ignoring the track off right. (But turn right here for Short walk 1, and note that this track is also used later in the course of the main walk, as the return route.) Bico Alto is reached two minutes later, as you emerge on a surfaced road (where you turn left, if you are doing Short walk 2).

Cross directly over the road and join the track opposite. It leads sharp left, briefly parallel to the road. This is the start of a panoramic high-level ridge walk through a number of cork oak plantations. Keep ahead on this wide stabilised track, ignoring tracks off to the right, and enjoy views over the northern countryside, shown on page 119. The pink heather, *Erica australis*, provides a touch of colour in places, but most of the interest lies in the vastness of the rolling landscape — emphasised by a solitary umbrella pine, *Pinus pinea*, by the side of the track. Almost immediately after passing a breeze-block hut on the left (**1h12min**), turn down a minor track on the left, to start to descend from the ridge. After just three minutes, turn left through two very grand gateposts which stand in splendid isolation in the middle of nowhere, striding over the low chain if it is in position, to continue along a narrow track. As the track swings right (**1h17min**), go left onto a very rough field track, continuing along a small ridge and heading roughly in the direction of Bico Alto. In **1h22min**, just before reaching a small summit where the track dies, turn left by two boundary marker stones, to follow a vague path with cistus to the left and a cleared area to the right. Follow the faint path along a ridge, using a line of half-metre-high boundary marker stones as a guide. At the second of these, reached two minutes later, turn sharp right and head straight down to the lower edge of a cork oak plantation — without the guidance of a path. Turn left at the bottom, on meeting a faint path; it leads in diagonal descent towards a streambed, reached in **1h26min**. Cross the dry streambed to the right, and continue on a path diagonally left; it rises to join a field track almost immediately. Keep ahead in **1h32min**, ignoring the track off left. It's a steady climb back to the main road (**1h37min**, where Short walk 2 joins from left).

Turn right to follow the surfaced road which promptly runs into track and starts to descend. Views soon open up on the left, to reveal a river snaking its way along the bottom of the valley. In **1h48min**, as you reach a place where tracks join from both sides, turn left down the narrow track for about 20m/yds. Now, looking right, you can see a clear route to follow down to the river — even though there is no definite path. Take care as you descend over this stony terrain, especially down the final steep section. Turn left as you reach the river bank a minute later, and walk upriver, keeping to the edge of the cork oak plantation. On reaching a stream, (**1h54min**), cross it and then turn left onto the rough track leading alongside the stream and away from the river. As the track swings away from the stream two minutes later, continue ahead by crossing the stream and going up the other bank.

You will have to switch from one side of the stream to the other (watching out for grass snakes as you go), until a more definite path on the right-hand side is reached (**2h**). Start to leave the valley and, in **2h05min,** meet a rough track: turn right for a short but steep climb, with good views over the stream and valley you have just walked. As you near the top of this rise (after you pass the path on the right), you are back on a section of track you walked earlier. But not for long: at **2h11min**, as you reach the track with the well on the right, turn right on the pleasant tree-lined track. Ahead are views of Tareja. As you meet a wall on the left (**2h20min**), turn left to join a path, now with the wall on your right. You have rejoined the outward route (at the 37min-point); now retrace your steps to São Bras.

19 TAVIRA NATIONAL FOREST

Distance: 8.0km/5mi; 1h46min

Grade: easy-moderate. The walk, mainly on tracks, is fairly easy going, apart from a tricky descent to cross the river towards the end. The only significant climbing is up to the trig point.

Equipment: sturdy shoes or boots, long-sleeved shirt, long trousers, sunglasses, suncream, cardigan, raingear, picnic, water

How to get there and return: 🚗 only accessible by car. Travelling eastwards from the Faro direction, look for the large hotel 'Eurotel', some 3km/1.9mi beyond the new bridge at Tavira. Turn left 300m beyond the hotel, along a road signposted 'Pension' and — less obviously — 'Mata Nacional' (National Forest). Swing right soon, to cross the bridge over the stream, and continue ahead, ignoring roads off to the right. The parking area is reached 4km/2.5mi further on, as you pass between gateposts and come to an open area with a house up to the left.

Shorter walks: All require the same equipment as above.

1 5km/3.1mi; 1h05min; easy. Use the notes for the main walk to pass through the cutting (27min). Then look out for the path on the left, reached 2 minutes later — just before a ruin on the right. Follow this along a winding valley, soon crossing the stream, to continue with it on your right. The path is a bit overgrown, but easily passable. In seven minutes you rise up to a track; cross it to join a track joining directly opposite. Go down this grassy track. In 17 minutes you reach the outward route at the ford, from where you return to your car.

2 5.7km/3.5mi; 1h10min; easy-moderate. Follow the main walk to the cutting (27min); then take the track off right immediately beyond it. Continue up this track for six minutes, until you reach another track entering from the left. Here you rejoin the main walk; pick up those notes (at the 51min-point). An optional diversion (add 1km/0.6mi; 20min) to the trig point is reached six minutes later.

3 6.5km/4.0mi; 1h20min; easy. Follow the main walk until you reach the track junction in 51min. Then turn right, instead of left and, a minute later, take the track on the left. Within ten minutes this takes you down to the river ford first reached 16min into the main walk. From here retrace your steps back to the car.

4 7km/4.3mi; 1h26min; easy-moderate. Follow the main walk, but leave out the diversion to the trig point (at the 57min-point).

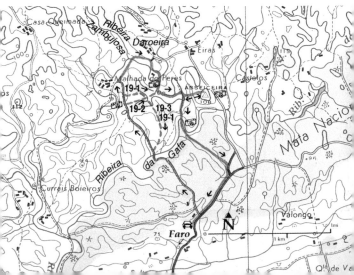

The Mata Nacional is not the grand forest region that its name suggests, but merely a fairly large plantation of eucalyptus trees. Our walk quickly takes you through and out of the forest into the pleasing countryside beyond. The *matos*-covered hills hiding small villages seem to roll timelessly away, creating an extremely photogenic landscape, given a clear day and a touch of colour. Panoramic views from the trig point make this diversion well worth the effort involved.

Start out from the car park by continuing along the surfaced road. After **3min** turn left, to join a track leading through the eucalyptus trees, and keep ahead at the junction of tracks reached in **7min**. Now in gentle descent, the track soon winds down to the ford over the Ribeira da Gafa (**16min**). Cross on stones and continue on the track beyond (the return route for Short walks 1 and 3 is the grassy track on the right here). Follow the main track up from the river, leaving the forest behind, to enjoy more open views. If you look to the right, you will see the trig point perched on top of Asseiceira at 108m/355ft; this is visited later in the walk. There is some climbing involved now, until you reach a cutting (**27min**). Beyond here you get your first real taste of the panoramic views which can be enjoyed throughout much of the rest of the walk.

The track off right beyond the cutting is the route of Short walk 2, but the main walk keeps straight ahead, enjoying views over the village of Malhada, which can be seen below to the left (photograph on the next page). The track leads past some ruins on the left some two minutes later (Short walk 3 leaves the main walk just before these ruins, along the path to the right).A junction of tracks is reached in **34min**. Turn right here, passing a round hut on the right, and heading towards the village of Daroeira, which soon comes into view. Continue ahead, in **39min**, where a small river, the Ribeira da Zambujosa, crosses the track (use the stepping stones). Then turn right at the track junction reached a minute later. Daroeira is close by on the left now, but it is soon left behind, when you bear right at the next track junction (**43min**). A brief ascent here sees you climbing above the River Zambujosa, which is now on the right, only to descend to re-cross it in **46min**.

The walk takes on a different pastoral ambience for a time, as you climb steeply away from the river. Looking back as you ascend, there are some fine views over the village of Daroeira. Turn left when you meet another track at the top of the hill (**51min**; but go right for Short walk 3).

From beyond the cutting reached in 27min, you start to obtain the fine views that characterise this walk. Below lies the village of Malhada.

You enjoy more good views from this high level track. As you near the trig point on Asseiceira, turn right (**57min**) onto a rough track, heading down between two carob trees. The diversion to the trig point starts as you reach these carobs. From here descend the narrow gully to the left, in the direction of the trig point, taking great care over the stony ground. From the bottom of the gully, head up for the trig point, taking the line between the *matos* on the right and the almond grove on the left. From the trig point reached in **1h17min**, there is a fantastic panorama to absorb.

Return to the two carob trees by the side of the track when you are ready, and continue the walk by heading down the rough track towards the sea. As you descend into the valley, the stony track peters out and continues as a path. Where the path divides, go left towards a saddle, which is reached in **1h21min**. There is no defined path leading down to the river from here, but that is the way we need to go, in order to join the track which can be seen on the far side of the river. Leave the saddle by going down the bank, towards the loop in the river, reached four minute later. Then go left along the river, to descend to water level, before heading back right to find a crossing point (use available stones or the fallen tree spanning the river as a bridge). Climb the river bank to reach the track, and head back into the eucalyptus forest. When you join the surfaced road (**1h38min**), turn right and soon reach a junction, where you turn right again. This road leads back to the car park, reached eight minutes later.

20 CASTRO MARIM NATURE RESERVE

Distance: 11.6km/7.2mi; 2h10min

Grade: moderate. This walk does not have the relaxation of undulations; it is constantly on the level, which can be very tiring over a long distance. A section of footpath near the end of the walk demands some agility.

Equipment: sturdy shoes or boots, long-sleeved shirt, long trousers, binoculars, sunglasses, suncream, cardigan, raingear, picnic, water

How to get there: 🚐 by bus from Faro to Vila Real de Santo António. Journey time 1h50min normal service (Timetable 8) or 1h10min express service (Timetable 8a). Then take a taxi to Castro Marim (a short journey of 3km). When you turn off the main EN125 just outside Vila Real, the start of the walk is on the left, 1.6km along this road — before the first vineyard, also on the left. 🚆 by train from Faro to Vila Real. Journey time, depending on the number of stops, from 1h18min to 1h44min TImetable 11). Then take a taxi (a short journey of 3km). 🚗 by car: Castro Marim lies just to the northwest of Vila Real; see Car tour 4 for details of how to get there. Park by the road, or by the ruined building down the track to the left, some 1.6km/1mi after turning north onto the EN122 from the main EN125 immediately outside Vila Real.

To return: Walk to Castro Marim and, from there, return by taxi for your bus or train (Timetables 8, 8a, 11) from Vila Real to Faro.

Shorter walk: 9.8km/6.1mi; 1h45min; same grade and equipment as above. Follow the main walk as far as the gate across the track and return the same way. This has the advantage of avoiding the more difficult path at the later stage of the walk, while still seeing the best of the reserve.

Although the walk starts just to the south of Castro Marim, it is well worth having a look around the town — either before you start out or at the end of the walk. If you are travelling by public transport, save this until the end of the walk, so that you can take a taxi back from there to Vila Real. The castle dominating the town is believed to have its origins back in Roman times, but was the seat of the Knights of Christ in the 14th century until this was transferred to Tomar. The earthquake of 1755 largely

destroyed the castle, although parts still remain, and the present castle was built by King Afonso III. You can stroll around inside to inspect the old walls and enjoy its commanding location, looking over the Rio Guardiana towards Ayamonte in Spain. There is a centre within the castle where you can obtain more information on the nature reserve, which is illustrated on wall maps.

The nature reserve itself covers the area of *salinas* south and east of the town. *Salinas* are the production units used to obtain sea salt. They are flooded with sea water which is allowed to evaporate under the influence of the sun and the strong coastal winds, until the salt finally crystallises out. With its long hot summers, Algarve is an ideal location for salt production by this method, and its history dates back more than 2500 years, from the time when salt was first produced for preserving fish. Castro Marim was a particularly important centre for this activity, and a 1791 survey revealed that there were 185 active *salinas* in this region alone. They are vastly reduced in numbers now, but those that remain are valuable sites for wild life, especially for wading birds and waterfowl. This walk will delight the bird-watchers particularly, and the birds that you can expect to see, depending on the season, include flamingos, *Phoenicopterus ruber*, in a large flock, the lovely black-winged stilt, *Himantopus himantopus*, which is the symbol of this reserve, the white stork, *Ciconia ciconia*, and a variety of other birds which we are not skilled enough to identify. The list of known visitors to the reserve is too long to quote in full, but includes a number of sandpipers like the dunlin, *Calidris alpina*; plovers like the ringed plover, *Charadrius hiaticula*, and the avocet, *Recurvirostra avosetta*.

The route of the walk as described is the *only* circular route in the reserve, and it is not possible to short-cut the circuit by using the banks that divide the *salinas*. Any attempt to do this may be dangerous and will result in you retracing your steps.

Start the walk from the main road just south of Castro Marim (22 minutes' walking time from the centre) and 1.6km/1mi north of the EN125. Take the track heading west, which runs on the south side of a vineyard. A ruined building on the left is passed in **3min**, as you head out towards the *salinas*. From here the river over to the left becomes more noticeable. At the point where the course of the river swings away to the left (**11min**), note that the path on the left is the return route. Olive and carob groves on the right add colour and contrast to the flatness of the *salinas* now on the left. The flamingos are usually in a large flock, so they are easily seen across the emptiness of the large lagoons. Stay with the main track, as you swing around right, to get good views of Castro Marim (the photograph on pages 32-33 was taken here). The closest point to the castle is reached in **24min**, as you swing left on meeting the river. Keep following the main track, keeping

These large salinas (production units used to obtain sea salt) are near the start of the walk. The flock of flamingos is often seen here but, if they are too frequently disturbed by visitors, they move to the quieter western parts of the reserve. No matter where they are, if you complete the circuit, you should see them at some point in the walk.

an eye open for the wading birds in some of the shallower parts. As the sun gets stronger the storks take to the wing, and they can be seen lazily circling and rising on the thermals.

The salt plant is approached in **42min** and is now over to the left. Stay with the track, to reach a cross-track in **53min**, where there is a gate diagonally across the track. Keep ahead, passing through the gateway. From here the track winds its way through dykes — full on the right, but dry on the left. Vila Real fills the skyline ahead for a time but, as you swing left, Castro Marim comes back into view.

Follow the track towards a white building (a pumping station), which is reached in **1h27min**. Here turn left, to walk along the top of a dyke, with the river close by on the right, and the railway just over the river. For a time you might wonder if you are on the right route, since the path is quite overgrown, and the bank is just a mass of bright yellow Bermuda buttercups (*Oxalis pes-caprae*; see photograph page 38). Again, you might wonder, when you see the very good track running parallel on the next embankment to the left … but rest assured that, if you stay by the riverside, this path connects up to your outward route.

Keep following the banks of the river, taking the line of least resistance, in the parts where the path gets particularly overgrown. It is not difficult to walk, but care is required with the footwork from time to time. Note that, in

1h50min, the good track over on the left swings away to head for the salt plant, whereas our path meets a broad path two minutes later, where you turn right to head back to join the outward track. A sharp right turn, when you meet the track (**1h59min**), leads you back to the road.

At 20 minutes into the walk, looking just a short distance away, you can see familiar farmland crops, like the almond trees shown here. It's very different from the vegetation growing close to the salinas, where only salt-tolerant plants like the glassworts (Arthrocnemem sp) and the saltworts (Salicoria sp) can survive.

BUS AND TRAIN TIMETABLES

There are two bus companies operating in Algarve. The Rodoviaria Nacional EP is the larger company, which operates local services all over the region — as well as the long distance services to Lisbon, Porto and other major towns. Their buses, in orange livery, bear the initials RN. The other company, Castelo & Cacorino, runs blue/grey buses marked with C&C. This company operates only in the region of Lagoa and points west. Generally, there are printed timetables available for many of the RN services, obtained at the major bus depots and at some tourist information offices, but this facility did not seem to extend to the C&C buses. Their timetables are posted in the offices of the company and often at terminals and other major bus stops.

Remember that bus timetables are liable to change without notice, so always be sure to check the times of your bus. Do not rely solely on the timetables reproduced here. Buses are not numbered, but the final destination is displayed on the front, so be sure to check before you board.

For some bus journeys it is necessary to book a ticket before you board, particularly when you board at a bus station; for others you pay on the bus. On some journeys there is a 15 per cent discount if you book a return ticket. If you are setting out on a long-distance journey, it is normal to book in advance. If your accommodation is not near a bus station, you can book through a nearby travel agency. The tourist office will advise you of the nearest.

In the list below, the numbers following place names refer to **bus timetable numbers** (except for 11, which is a **train timetable**). The train is considerably cheaper than the bus but, be warned, it is often much slower.

Albufeira 7, 9, 10, 11
Albufeira station 10, 11
Almancil 9
Armação de Pêra 9
Burgau 1
Caldas de Monchique 3
Estói 6
Faro 6, 8, 8a, 9, 11
Ferreiras 9
Lagoa 4, 5, 9
Lagos 1, 2, 9, 11
Luz 1
Monchique 3

Montechoro 9
Paderne 7
Portimao 3, 4, 5, 9, 11
Praia da Rocha 9
Quarteira 9
Sagres 2
Salema 2
São Bras de Alportel 6
Silves 4, 5, 11
Tavira 8a, 11
Torralta 9
Vilamoura 9
Vila Real de SA 8, 8a, 11

Timetables begin on the next page.

1 Lagos — Luz — Burgau (C&C)

	Departure times *weekdays*	*Sundays*
Lagos	07.55, 08.55, 10.50, 13.15	09.35, 14.05
Luz	08.06, 09.06, 11.01, 13.26	09.46, 14.16
Burgau	08.14, 09.14, 11.09, 13.33	09.54, 14.24
Burgau	07.31, 08.21, 09.44, 11.27, 17.45	07.29, 10.05, 14.30
Luz	07.38, 08.28, 08.37, 09.51, 11.34, 17.52	07.36, 10.12, 14.37
Lagos	07.50, 08.30, 08.48, 10.02, 11.45, 18.04	07.52, 10.24, 14.49

2 Lagos — Salema — Sagres (RN)*

	Departure times *weekdays*	*Sundays*
Lagos	09.15, 11.05, 15.15, 18.25, 19.30	09.15, 11.05, 20.35
Salema	09.47, 11.37, 15.47, 18.57, 20.02	09.47, 11.37, 21.06
Sagres	10.02, 12.10, 16.20, 19.30, 10.35	10.02, 12.10, 21.40
Sagres	08.25, 18.20	19.40
Salema	08.59, 18.53	20.13
Lagos	09.30, 19.25	20.45

*The above is an extract from the Lagos — Sagres timetable, listing only the buses calling at Salema. The full timetable lists many more buses which ply the route between Lagos and Sagres and which stop at the crossroads outside Salema. This leaves a walk of 2km/1.25mi along the road to get into Salema, less than 25min walking time.

3 Portimão to Monchique (C&C)

	Departure times (daily)
Portimão	08.55, 10.15, 11.25, 14.20, 17.02, 18.05, 19.30
Caldas de Monchique	09.35, 10.55, 12.05, 15.00, 17.45, 18.54, 20.10
Monchique	09.50, 11.10, 12.20, 15.15, 18.00, 19.00, 20.25
Monchique	07.15, 08.45, 10.00, 12.45, 15.05, 15.35, 18.15
Caldas de Monchique	07.30, 08.58, 10.15, 13.00, 15.20, 15.50, 18.30
Portimão	08.10, 09.40, 10.55, 13.40, 16.00, 16.30, 17.10

4 Portimão to Silves (C&C)

	Departure times (daily)
Portimão	08.55, 12.00, 15.50, 17.30, 19.10
Lagoa	09.13, 12.18, 16.08, 17.48, 19.28
Silves	09.32, 12.37, 16.27, 18.07, 19.47
Silves	08.05, 09.00, 11.08, 15.00, 18.08
Lagoa	08.22, 09.20, 11.25, 15.17, 18.25
Portimão	08.45, 09.40, 11.45, 15.35, 18.45

5 Portimão — Silves (RN)

Departure times (daily)

Portimão	09.35, 11.30, 14.00, 16.30, 18.35
Lagoa	09.58, 09.58, 11.53, 14.26, 16.53, 18.58
Silves	10.10, 12.05, 14.38, 17.05, 19.10
Silves	07.30, 08.30, 10.30, 13.20, 14.45, 17.50
Lagoa	07.45, 08.45, 10.45, 13.35, 15.00, 18.05
Portimão	08.05, 11.05, 13.55, 15.20, 18.25

6 Faro — Estói — São Bras (RN)

Departure times (weekdays)

Faro	Estói	São Bras de Aportel arrive	Aportel depart	Estói	Faro
07.45	08.05	08.20	07.00	07.21	07.42
09.00	09.15a	09.27	—	07.25	07.46
10.30	10.50	11.05	07.15	07.30a	07.50
12.08	12.33	—	08.15	08.30	08.50
12.35	12.57	13.12	—	08.25	08.47
13.15	13.30d	13.42	09.50	10.05	10.25
13.35	14.00	14.15	11.33	11.43a	12.00
16.39	16.50	17.05	—	13.30	13.50
17.05	17.23	—	13.25	13.40a	13.59
17.10	17.28a	17.38	14.15	14.30	14.50
17.30	17.52	—	15.30	15.45	16.05
18.15	18.35	18.50	17.08	17.20a	17.35
18.35	18.57	19.18	—	17.55	18.17
18.50	19.09a	19.20	18.10	18.25	18.45
19.15	19.37	—	—	19.40	20.00
19.20	19.39a	19.50			

Departure times (weekends)

Faro	Estói	São Bras de Aportel arrive	Aportel depart	Estói	Faro
07.45b	08.05b	08.20	—	07.25	07.45
09.00	09.15a	09.27	07.15	07.30a	07.50
12.35	12.50a	13.02	—	08.25b	08.49
13.35b	13.54ab	14.08	09.50b	10.05b	10.25
16.30	16.50	17.05	13.10c	13.25c	13.45
18.50	19.15	19.30	13.40b	13.55	14.15
			17.08	17.20a	17.35
			19.38	19.50a	20.05

a bus does not enter Estói, but stops at the crossroads about 1km away
— convenient both for visiting the Roman ruins and for Walk 16
b Saturdays only
c Sundays only

7 Albufeira — Paderne (RN)

Departure times (daily)

Albufeira	07.40, 10.50b, 12.30a, 13.30a, 13.40, 16.45a, 17.50, 18.50
Paderne	08.08, 11.18, 12.58, 13.58, 14.08, 17.13, 18.18, 19.18
Paderne	08.10, 09.20a, 12.35b, 13.05a, 14.15a, 14.45, 17.50a, 18.20
Albufeira	08.38, 09.48, 13.03, 13.33, 14.43, 15.13, 18.18, 18.48

a except Saturdays and Sundays
b except Sundays and holidays

8   Faro — Vila Real SA (RN; journey time 1h50min)

Departure times from Faro (daily)
07.30, 09.10, 11.00, 12.40a, 13.15, 15.00, 16.30a, 17.40, 18.40a, 19.40b

Departure times from Vila Real de Santo António (daily)
07.30, 08.40a, 09.50, 11.05, 12.40, 14.35, 16.05a, 17.20, 18.30
a except Saturday, Sunday and national holidays
b only on Saturday, Sunday and national holidays

8a   Faro — Vila Real SA (RN; express service using the Lisbon bus; journey time 1h10min)

	Departure times (daily)
Faro	06.20, 10.00, 13.00, 19.00, 21.20
Tavira	06.55, 10.35, 13.35, 19.35, 21.55
Vila Real	07.30, 11.10, 14.10, 20.10, 22.30
Vila Real	06.15, 07.30, 11.00, 15.45, 17.45
Tavira	06.50, 08.05, 11.35, 16.20, 18.20
Faro	07.25, 08.40, 12.10, 16.55, 18.55

9   Faro — Albufeira — Portimão — Lagos (RN; express)

Other services ply this route; remember to check those timetables.

	Departure times
Faro	07.30, 09.10, 14.40, 18.00
Almancil	07.43, 09.23, 14.53, 18.13
Quarteira	07.54, 09.34, 15.04, 18.24
Vilamoura	07.57, 09.37, 15.07, 18.27
Montechoro	08.22, 10.02, 15.32, 18.52
Albufeira	08.28, 10.08, 15.38, 18.58
Ferreiras	08.35, 10.15, 15.45, 19.05
Armação de Pêra	08.49, 10.29, 15.59, 19.19
Lagoa	08.59, 10.39, 16.09, 19.29
Portimão	09.10, 10.50, 16.20, 19.40
Praia da Rocha	09.13, 10.53, 16.23, 19.43
Torralta	09.24, 11.04, 16.34, 19.54
Lagos	09.44, 11.24, 16.54, 19.54
Lagos	07.15, 10.00, 14.30, 17.10
Torralta	07.36, 10.21, 14.51, 17.31
Praia da Rocha	10.31, 15.01, 17.41
Portimão	07.47, 10.34, 15.04, 17.44
Lagoa	07.58, 10.45, 15.15, 17.55
Armação de Pêra	08.06, 10.56, 15.26, 18.06
Ferreiras	08.20, 11.12, 15.42, 18.22
Albufeira	—, 11.19, 15.49, 18.29
Montechoro	—, 11.24, 15.54, 18.34
Vilamoura	—, 11.49, 16.19, 18.59
Quarteira	—, 11.53, 16.23, 19.03
Almancil	—, 12.04, 16.34, 19.14
Faro	08.52, 12.15, 16.45, 19.25

10 Albufeira — Albufeira station (RN; journey time 15min)

Depart Albufeira (daily)
06.55, 07.15, 08.15, 09.15, 10.05, 10.50, 12.10, 13.05, 14.05,
15.10, 16.35, 17.00, 17.50, 18.15, 19.15, 20.00, 22.15

Depart station (daily)
07.10, 07.35, 08.15, 08.40, 09.45, 10.30, 11.35, 12.40, 13.45,
14.35, 16.05, 17.00, 17.25, 18.10, 18.40, 19.45, 20.20, 23.30

11 Train timetable, Lagos — Vila Real

This is an extract from the full timetable which is extensive and
available free of charge from most railway stations and some tourist
offices. All the trains departures are listed but only for a selection of
stations.

Lagos	Portimão	Silves	Albufeira	Faro	Tavira	V Real
—	—	—	05.42	06.24	07.07	07.48
—	—	—	06.29	07.38	08.34	09.22
06.22	06.57	07.18	07.50	08.56	09.43	10.17
07.28	07.58	08.18	09.12	10.11	11.05	11.50
08.10	08.47	09.08	10.25	11.57	12.39	13.15
10.10	10.45	11.06	11.51	12.40	—	—
12.10	12.44	13.06	13.50	14.45	15.37	16.21
13.55	14.25	14.45	15.25	16.13	16.59	17.40
15.03	15.35	15.55	16.33	17.25	18.24	19.12
—	—	—	—	18.41	19.27	20.02
16.20	16.49	17.11	—	—	—	—
17.45	18.13	18.33	19.16	20.01	20.45	21.23
18.50	19.24	19.46	20.31	21.18	22.09	22.41
20.40	21.15	21.37	22.14	22.57	23.48	00.30
22.24	22.57	23.10	—			—

VReal	Tavira	Faro	Albufeira	Silves	Portimão	Lagos
—	—	—	—	06.04	06.22	06.56
—	—	—	—	06.59	07.20	07.54
04.50	05.34	06.31	07.29	08.20	08.45	09.20
07.08	07.52	08.49	09.37	10.28	10.48	11.15
08.48	09.23	10.06	10.53	11.47	12.06	12.40
10.17	10.51	11.48	12.50	13.34	13.53	14.19
—	—	13.00	13.49	14.44	15.03	15.37
12.13	12.58	13.45	—	—	—	—
13.49	14.25	15.15	16.13	16.52	17.13	17.45
15.43	16.20	17.15	17.49	19.00	19.21	19.50
17.40	18.23	19.13	20.10	20.50	21.12	21.44
18.34	19.26	20.29	21.28	22.35	22.55	23.21
20.02	20.47	21.45	22.41	23.48	00.06	00.32
21.40	22.12	23.00	23.40			

🌻 Index

Geographical names comprise the only entries in this index. For subject entries, please refer to the Contents, page 3. *Italic* type indicates a map reference; **bold face** type a photograph or drawing. Both of these may be in addition to a text reference on the same page.